The DeQueen & Eastern Railroad: History Through the Miles

Barton Jennings

Publisher's Cataloging-in-Publication Data
Jennings, Barton

The DeQueen & Eastern Railroad: History Through the Miles
296p.; 21cm.
ISBN: 979-8-9904307-2-3
Library of Congress Control Number: 2025933653

Front cover photos by Barton Jennings.
Back cover photo by Sarah Jennings.
All interior photos by Barton Jennings unless otherwise noted.

Please send comments or corrections to sarah@techscribes.com

TechScribes, Inc.
PO Box 2199
Alma, AR 72921
www.techscribes.com

Printed in the United States of America

Contents

Other books by Barton Jennings

Acknowledgments

The author has been fortunate enough to know some of the employees who worked for the DeQueen & Eastern Railroad over the years, and was involved in the centennial event held by the company September 29-October 1, 2000. Additionally, he has had the pleasure to get to know a number of the people who have researched the railroad, such as Arkansas railroad historian Bill Pollard. All of these deserve a thanks.

A number of documents were also used in writing this book. It is amazing what can be found on the internet these days. Copies of the *Official Guide*, the annual reports of various state railroad and corporation commissions, Interstate Commerce Commission reports, and other such documents were great resources.

Related sources such as the *Arkansas Marketing and Industrial Guide*, *The Coal Dealers Blue Book*, local histories published by the Goodspeed Publishing Company, Sanborn Insurance Maps, the many lumber trade magazines, and others were a great aid. Newspapers also reported on the construction and operations of the railroads owned by the Dierks brothers. David Hoge is a master of newspaper research. His collection of more than 3000 pages of railroad-related newspaper articles from Arkansas is a masterful source of information, and he deserves a thanks for sharing this resource. The digital newspapers available through the Library of Congress were also valuable. An excellent book about the logging industry in the Ouachita Mountains is *Sawmill* by Kenneth L. Smith. The book provides a good background on the various logging companies that operated in the area, including those related to the Dierks family.

Finally, the author has a house with several rooms full of books, timetables and other documents about this and other railroads – important research items from a time long before today's internet. All of these and more were used in producing this volume.

This photo at Dierks, Arkansas, shows about 20 boxcars being loaded with lumber from the Dierks Lumber & Coal Company sawmill. The boxcars came from railroads like the New York Central; Gulf, Mobile & Ohio; Southern Pacific, and others. *American Lumberman*, December 25, 1920, page 106. The December 25, 1920, issue of *American Lumberman* featured more than 40 pages about Dierks Lumber. The article, entitled "A Pictorial Story of Arkansas and Oklahoma Soft Pine and Hardwoods and Their Conversion into Lumber by the Dierks Lumber & Coal Co., Kansas City, Mo." was actually designated by the magazine as "Advertisement" under the provisions of the Postal Act of August 20, 1912. Apparently, the article was written for Dierks Lumber as part of a promotional program celebrating the completion of the railroads and a number of improvements at its various sawmills.

Creating a DeQueen & Eastern Railroad Route Guide

This book is designed to provide a guide to the former Dierks railroads of the DeQueen & Eastern and Texas, Oklahoma & Eastern, and what is still there today. It is based upon materials created for the railroad's centennial and follows the combined railroad from Milepost 0.0 at Valliant, Oklahoma, eastward to the end of the railroad at Milepost 87.0 at Perkins, Arkansas. Each station and many of the waterways crossed by the two railroads are described, along with their own histories and stories.

The DeQueen & Eastern and Texas, Oklahoma & Eastern have operated as one ever since they were connected near the Arkansas-Oklahoma State Line on January 5, 1921, with full operations beginning a few months later. The 1921 issue of *Poor's Manual of Railroads* reported on the event.

The extension of the DeQueen & Eastern RR, west from De Queen, Ark., to the Arkansas-Oklahoma State Line, a distance of approximately 9.08 miles, which connects with the extension of the Texas, Oklahoma & Eastern RR, east from Broken Bow, Okla., a distance of approximately 15.67 miles to the Oklahoma-Arkansas State Line, was completed and placed in operation May 14, 1921.

DE QUEEN & EASTERN RAILROAD CO.

TEXAS, OKLAHOMA & EASTERN RAILROAD CO.

SEVENTH FLOOR GATES BUILDING

The two railroads – the DeQueen & Eastern and Texas, Oklahoma & Eastern – had their names on stationary used by Dierks Lumber & Coal in 1920, even before the two lines were connected. Courtesy of Sevier County Museum, Keith McKinney Collection.

The two railroads were originally built to connect the timber to the mills of the Dierks family, and then the lumber and wood products to the national market. The control of the railroads by Dierks continued until September 1969 when Weyerhaeuser acquired the timber, mills, and railroads. Weyerhaeuser made many changes, opening and closing mills, and buying, selling and trading timberlands. The railroads were sold to Patriot Rail in 2010, creating the DeQueen and Eastern Railroad, LLC (generally still shown as DeQueen & Eastern), which assumed control of the entire rail operation.

The DeQueen & Eastern and the Texas, Oklahoma & Eastern, have long been operated as one railroad system. This AAR-DOT grade crossing sign at Felker, Oklahoma, shows that both railroad names – DQE/TOE – are used interchangeably.

Even with these changes, much of the railroad's history can still be found along its route. There are several museums along the line, a station and bridges, and lots of trains that can still be photographed. The mainline between Valliant and Perkins is still in service, but the logging lines and many of the mill tracks are now retired, with few traces in some cases.

There is always the question about how much detail to provide in a book like this. One reader told the author that in a previous book, if someone once tied a mule to a she-shed along the line, it was reported. While that is not quite the goal, there is an effort to explain the history of each community along the line, what shippers were located there, and what facilities the railroad had. Obviously, all of these changed over the one hundred plus years of the railroad's history, so the challenge is how much information to report. In writing this book, the author attempted to include information about the first few years of the railroad's existence, the peak of a community's activity, and what remains today. Not everything is reported, but enough history is provided to give the reader an idea of what happened at each location.

The railroad historically used east-west as the line's description, although in some areas it curves greatly from these directions. The route description will use the east-west railroad directions, but will often use the real directions when describing certain features along the route. Additionally, the tracks were often described by their car-lengths. These car-lengths varied over the years, but were generally around 45 feet per car during the first half of the twentieth century, and 55 feet per car during the latter part. Therefore a track listed as being 20 cars in length could hold about 900 feet of train before 1950, and a track cited as holding 15 cars later was the same length.

Another help in following the railroad and knowing what was at various locations are the many maps available on the internet. County road maps, topographic (topo) maps, and many other maps from the era can be found. Comparing these older maps with newer maps can often make finding the railroad easier. One map site that was very helpful while following the railroad is provided by the U.S. Geological Survey, which has been very active making their Historical Topographic Map Collection available through USGS TopoView.

Another issue deals with all of the names that were used to represent the railroad and its owners over the past one-hundred-plus years. Early records and reports often simply used the term Dierks railroad. This was due to the ownership of the operating railroad, and some of the track being built by the lumber company before being assigned to the railroads. The Texas, Oklahoma & Eastern was often cited as being the DeQueen & Eastern Railroad, although it was a separate company, but owned by the DQ&E. There is also the question about the spelling of DeQueen in the railroad's name. While the City of De Queen uses a space between parts of its name, the railroad has historically not done so, something supported by numerous Interstate Commerce Commission and Surface Transportation Board documents.

Additionally, an ampersand (&) will be used in railroad company names to make them easier to identify. Especially with companies like the DeQueen & Eastern, mixing the railroad name, the cities that it served, and the directions that it runs, can get very confusing. Therefore, even if the firm did not use or always use an ampersand, one will be used in this book to identify railroad names.

To simplify the issue, the term DeQueen & Eastern will often be used, but an effort has been made to be precise as to the actual owner based upon the era being discussed.

Another issue is the actual initials used by the railroads. DQ&E has been commonly used for most of the railroad's existence, but the actual initials generally used by the railroad have been D&E. This was true in 1914 when Dierks reported the use of D&E on equipment assigned to the DeQueen & Eastern, and TO&E for those assigned to the Texas, Oklahoma & Eastern. Today, the AAR reporting marks are DQE for the new DeQueen & Eastern. The Texas, Oklahoma & Eastern has used the initials TO&E, but has TOE as its current reporting marks. The abbreviations DQ&E and TO&E will generally be used throughout this book since they are probably more recognized by the general public.

Please forgive these and any other simplifications used in this book.

All along the railroad between Valliant and Perkins, these No Trespassing signs have been installed by Patriot Rail since its purchase of the line in late 2010.

The Dierks Lumber & Coal Company

The railroads at De Queen – the DeQueen & Eastern Railroad and the Texas, Oklahoma & Eastern Railroad – are the work of the Dierks brothers and their efforts to log the Ouachita Mountains around Southwest Arkansas and Southeast Oklahoma. For almost the entire history of the two railroads their core responsibility was to move the timber products required and produced by the Dierks Lumber & Coal Company and the Choctaw Lumber Company, their owners. Later, the railroads became owned by Dierks Forests, and then Weyerhaeuser. Today, they are owned by Patriot Rail.

This Patriot Rail sign for the DeQueen and Eastern Railroad stands near the railroad's office at De Queen, Arkansas.

The Dierks Lumber & Coal Company was a major factor in the development of De Queen, and much of southwest Arkansas and southeast Oklahoma. In 1909, it was declared that "by far the largest and most important single factor in the industrial development of Sevier county has been the Dierks Lumber and Coal Company."

The history of the company can be traced back to Hans Dierks, who was born in Germany in 1850. He and his parents moved to the United States in 1852 and settled in Iowa, after which Hans married and moved to western Iowa. During the early 1880s, the Dierks Brothers Company was founded by brothers Hans, Henry, Herman, and Peter Dierks, to sell lumber. As the company grew, it became the Dierks Lumber & Coal Company (generally using "and" instead of "&", but both were used) on April 3, 1895. It was headquartered in Lincoln, Nebraska, with retail yards in Juanita, Kenesaw and Broken Bow, Nebraska. While lumber was the primary business of the firm, it also sold coal as a heating fuel, thus the second part of the company's name. In 1897, the firm moved to Kansas City, Missouri, and bought out S. Z. Schutte's lumber company. Within a few years, the Dierks company had more than thirty retail yards in the Kansas City area, and was also selling lumber in Iowa and Nebraska.

One of the issues that the Dierks brothers ran into was obtaining a regular supply of quality lumber, and they began looking at acquiring their own timber and sawmills. In 1897, the company acquired a sawmill in Petros, Oklahoma, near Heavener, for $15,000. However, the mill closed three years later as the timber supply ran out. There were benefits from the mill as it introduced the brothers to the shortleaf pine in the Ouachita Mountains of Arkansas and Oklahoma.

The Ouachita Mountains originally contained what has been called the largest shortleaf pine forest in the world – five thousand square miles of the eleven thousand square mile Ouachita Mountains were covered by these trees. However, the trees grew very differently here, and the shortleaf pine often stood in open stands of widely spaced mature trees with a carpet of grass underneath. Little undergrowth existed due to fires caused by lightning, Indians, and early settlers. The majority of the trees were 12-28 inches in diameter, but most were less than 20 inches. Unlike some southern Mississippi areas that produced 10,000 or more board feet per acre, the Ouachita Mountains produced about 5000 board feet per acre, and required different logging and cutting methods.

In January 1900, three Dierks brothers (Hans, Herman, and Peter) acquired the Williamson Brothers Lumber Company operation at De Queen. The $60,000 purchase (some sources claim that it cost $250,000) included both a pine and a hardwood sawmill, dry kilns, a planing mill, timberlands, and a planned five-mile logging railroad that would extend east to the Cossatot River.

As part of the company's centennial in 2000, the De-Queen & Eastern Railroad published a short history of the company, and it stated that the railroad began in November of 1899 as the "DeQueen & Eastern Tram Railway," a planned logging tram for the Williamson Brothers Lumber Company. The DQ&E stated that at "the time of the purchase only the grading had been done for about three miles east of DeQueen." There were immediately reports that the logging railroad would be extended, and a local reporter asked Hans Dierks about building the logging tram. His response was, "No, we are going to build a broad-gauge railroad and will use heavy iron." The first iron rails arrived on the Kansas City, Pittsburg & Gulf Railroad (later known as the Kansas City Southern) on April 2, 1900, and the first load of logs was brought to the sawmill pond over the new tracks on May 25, 1900. The *De Queen Bee* had a front page article about this new activity in their June 1, 1900, issue.

Friday afternoon, the first load of logs shipped over the DeQueen & Eastern, was pulled by No. 9 and dumped into the large pool at the mill of Dierks Lumber & Coal Company. The result of Saturday's traffic was the delivery of about 40,000 feet of fine timber to the mill. Trains have been running every day since that time and will continue regularly.

A Bee *representative was informed by Mr. W. A. Prater that grading would resume just as soon as the road already built was in good running order.*

De Queen can count on having a railroad extending far into the eastern territory before the close of 1900.

With this start the company began to make plans to expand into the area, and Herman Dierks moved to De Queen in 1902 to lead the effort. As stated by several histories, over the next several decades, "the company came to operate more than twenty retail lumber yards, built and operated six lumber mills, built railroads, acquired at least twelve lumber manufacturing or timber companies, purchased over 1,250,000 acres of land, and implemented some of the first forestry conservation policies in the South. The Dierks family established a lumber dynasty that made their name a household word in the region." The timber in Arkansas and Oklahoma was a major part of this fame, advertised as "Dierks Superior Soft Pine."

The Dierks built up an impressive empire of companies throughout the region. These of course included the Dierks Lumber & Coal Company and the Choctaw Lumber Company, but also the Dierks & Sons Lumber Company, Dierks Tie & Timber Company, Dierks Investment Company, Pine Valley Lumber Company, Waterman Lumber & Supply Company, Sutherland Lumber Company, and Florien Lumber Company. Most of these firms were based in the offices of Dierks on the seventh floor of the Gates Building, located at 1006 Grand Boulevard, Kansas City, Missouri. The Gates Building was originally built by real estate developer Jemuel C. Gates in 1909. While the structure was designed to be built taller, it originally had only five stories, most of which were to be used for storage. However, office space soon became the primary purpose of the building, and the Dierks Lumber & Coal Company started renting space by 1915, requiring several more floors to be built. In 1925, Dierks leased the entire building and added eight floors. In 1927, the Dierks Investment Company bought the building, which became known as the Dierks Building. In 1930, two more floors were added, making a total of seventeen stories. During the Great Depression, only 35% of the building was occupied, and this decreased further through the 1940s and 1950s. In 1954, the Home Savings Association, which had been a tenant since 1945, bought the building for the Home Savings and Loan Company. The building then became known as the Home Savings Association Building. In 2009, the building was converted into the Grand Boulevard Lofts. Today, the building is listed on the National Register of Historic Places.

Among the timber acquired near De Queen were many acres in Oklahoma. Until the start of the twentieth century, the lands within the Choctaw Nation were owned by the tribe, and it was difficult to obtain large tracts of timber to harvest. The allotment process in the early 1900s took land from the Choctaw Nation and put it into private hands. Much of the land went to tribal members, but land that was not assigned could then be obtained by companies looking to cut the timber. With this change, lumbering went from independent and small companies using small steam and gasoline sawmills scattered throughout the backwoods, to large-scale lumbering and their steam and electric-driven mills. To operate the Oklahoma lumber operations, the Dierks created the Choctaw Lumber Company.

The first new mill built by Dierks was at the community of Dierks, Arkansas, in response to a series of storms that knocked down large volumes of their timber. The pine mill at De Queen burned on May 5, 1909, and was never rebuilt. The company later moved the hardwood mill and the planing mill from De Queen to Bismark (Wright City). A stave mill was also located at Bismark as well as Broken Bow during the 1910s. As the company's railroads expanded, new mills were built and new towns founded in several places along the lines. As the lumber activity grew, the firm ended its operation of lumberyards across the Midwest, selling to retail stores across the country.

While the focus of this book is on the railroad between Valliant, Oklahoma, and Perkins, Arkansas, it should be noted that not all of the company's logging operations were on this rail line. A number of timber operations were located miles away, and some were served by long logging spurs. During the years that Dierks operated in Oklahoma, the company had temporary logging towns set up at ten different locations, all on or near logging spurs that broke off from the Texas, Oklahoma & Eastern. Others were too far away, such as the towns and mills at Mountain Pine, Arkansas, and Garvin, Oklahoma. Each of these Dierks mills also had their own railroad spurs which used steam locomotives from the company's fleet.

The December 25, 1920, issue of *American Lumberman* had a 40 page article about Dierks Lumber & Coal. A large number of details about the various mills and some of the rail and logging operations were included in the article. It stated that at the time, the company had three pine mills – Broken Bow, Dierks, and Wright City – and a single hardwood mill at Broken Bow that handled oak, gum, sycamore, elm, cypress, maple hickory, and ash. While oxen had initially been used, by this time 4-mule teams were used to move logs to the railroad tracks, except for the hardwood logging at Broken Bow where a Lidgerwood overhead skidder worked a 1000-1200 foot radius area.

The article also stated that the company had 75 miles of logging spurs and the railroad used 16 locomotives, 130 forty-foot steel-underframe logging cars, and seven American log loaders. Many of these were maintained at the TO&E locomotive shops at Wright City. The railroad section gangs, track inspectors and foremen used 20 Fairbanks, Morse & Co. motor cars.

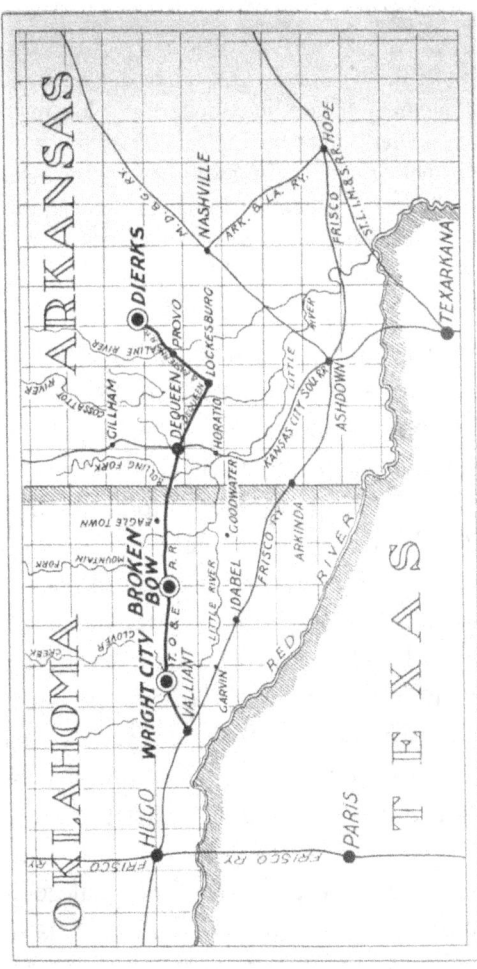

This map from the December 25, 1920, issue of the *American Lumberman* showed the De-Queen & Eastern and Texas, Oklahoma & Eastern railroads, as well as the sites of the major Dierks mills along the routes. *American Lumberman*, December 25, 1920, page 68.

This close-up of a photo from the 1920 article in *American Lumberman* shows one of the many 40-foot steel-underframe logging flat cars used by the railroads. Dierks kept buying cars like these, with announcements that it had bought 25 steel-underframe logging flat cars from the American Car & Foundry Company in 1925, and eight more flat cars in 1926 from the Mt. Vernon Car & Manufacturing Company.

Other reports from the time, and the following decade, provided additional information. The records of the Marion Steam Shovel Company show that the Dierks Lumber & Coal Company acquired two Barnhart Log Loaders, a small 360-degree swing crane used to load logs upon railcars. The Barnhart Log Loader actually ran on tracks that were mounted on the railcars, making train switching and log loading easier. Only 218 Barnharts were produced between 1886 and 1927, and those acquired by Dierks were the earlier model which in 1906 became known as the Model 10 Marion Loader. The company also used other types of loading equipment. For example, Dierks used a Lidgerwood Skidder for many years to load hardwood logs, but it was for sale by 1925.

Until the 1920s, Dierks Lumber & Coal generally sold off the land after it harvested the timber. This was a standard practice in the industry, known as "cut-and-run" or "cut and get out" logging, or some less favorable terms.

However, compared to most such plans, Dierks apparently worked to make sure that the sold land would become prosperous, producing more shipments for the railroad. In 1918, the *Broken Bow News* reported on the efforts, and the report was later picked up and used in the May 1918 issue of *Cut-Over Lands* magazine.

During the last few weeks, W. H. Jones, of the Immigration Department of the Texas, Oklahoma and Eastern Railroad, has sold more than 2,100 acres of well developed and improved farms, in tracts of from 80 to 160 acres. Four of these farms are complete with modern homes, barns and fences. A total of fourteen houses are now under construction on the other property sold. Besides selling farms improved ready for the plow, between here and Mountain Fork River, the railroad company has, through Mr. Jones, built a good road from Broken Bow to Mountain Fork, paralleling with the old Indian trail or military road, and is building roads along section lines south and east to Mountain Fork. These will be macadamed within a very short time. These highways run alongside some of the richest farm lands in the county, and touch Mountain Fork.

More reports about the efforts of William Henry Jones followed in the July 1918 issue of *Cut-Over Lands*. This issue included an interview of Mr. Jones and contained descriptions of the road building efforts, the operations of a 20-acre school farm where the production of different crops was demonstrated, and the requirements to participate in the land program. Jones provided a detailed description of the efforts as part of the article.

We are offering a wonderful opportunity to the poor man. We will allow him to select 160 acres of land, fence it for him with the best galvanized woven wire, build him a good four, five or six room house, a horse barn, cow barn and chicken house – starting him into business by furnishing him a home. With every house we build we furnish a well with a pump in the kitchen, also a sink with a drainage from the kitchen. We hang the shades in the houses. We even build chicken nests in the chicken houses and build walk-ways from the house to the road and lay off the front yards and sow in grass.

Good Farm Lands for Sale Cheap

Located in Sevier and Howard Counties, Ark., and McCurtain County, Okla.

We have thousands of acres of fine lands of the **Dierks Lumber & Coal Company** for sale to actual settlers who want good bottom or up-lands for agricultural purposes. These lands are especially adapted to the growing of corn, cotton, wheat, oats, rye, barley, sorghum, ribbon cane, millet, cow peas, peanuts, sweet and Irish potatoes, and all kinds of garden truck; all kinds of fruits and berries, including peaches, apples, pears, plums, blackberries, raspberries, dewberries and grapes.

Located near foothills of the Ozarks, health and climatic conditions are fine, thus making it an ideal place for a home.

We are offering these lands at exceedingly low prices and on terms that will enable any man to own his own farm.

Price: $5.00 to $15.00 per acre.

Terms: Small cash payment down, and balance in easy yearly payments.

For further information see or write:

FRED J. LEEPER,
Sales Agent,
De Queen, Ark.

JOHN CRAIG,
Sales Agent,
Broken Bow, Okla.

This advertisement from the January 1914 issue of *Current Events* offers land that the Dierks Lumber & Coal Company has logged – "Good Farm Lands for Sale Cheap." *Current Events* was published as a Kansas City Southern promotional magazine and was described as an industrial and agricultural magazine. *Current Events*, January 1914.

By 1915, the Dierks Lumber & Coal Company ads found in *Current Events* only promoted acres in Arkansas. *Current Events,* July 1915.

As the last of the existing forests were being cut, the company began to review its practices and started cutting second-growth timber. During this time, Dierks began to work with the United States Forest Service to educate the population about modern conservation of forests. Dierks also erected observation towers and helped to develop new firefighting tactics that reduced the damage wrought by forest fires.

A presentation at the 1929 National Safety Congress covered some of the safety efforts underway at Dierks Lumber & Coal and its subsidiaries. The talk stated that the company operated "five large pine mills, one hardwood mill, five logging camps, 100 miles of main line railroad, several hundred miles of logging railroad," and one general machine shop that served the various railroad operations.

The changes taking place in the industry led to a new charter of the company, becoming the new Dierks Lumber & Coal Company, incorporated in Delaware on November 29, 1929. The Great Depression of the 1930s ended many of the plans and the company entered receivership during October 1932, along with other lumber firms owned by the Dierks family: Choctaw Lumber Company and Pine Valley Lumber Company. The main company kept operating and was reorganized starting in 1934, absorbing the other lumber companies and leading to the creation of another new Dierks Lumber & Coal Company. Again, it was incorporated in Delaware, this time on January 4, 1936. At the time, the company operated pine mills along these railroads at Dierks, Arkansas; Broken Bow, Oklahoma; and Wright City, Oklahoma, and the Dierks' mills produced 60 percent of the lumber made in Oklahoma.

As the economy improved, the various Dierks mills reopened, and the Dierks family proudly paid off all of its debts by World War II. As a part of this effort, all of the lumber companies were folded into the Dierks Lumber & Coal Company. The company also made a change in its logging practices and began buying up cut land and employing a sustained yield program whereby cutting was rotated to allow trees to mature for fresh cutting. While the company was being modernized, not everything went smoothly. A two-month-long strike at Wright City, Clebit, and Broken Bow led to an eight-cent-per-hour pay increase in 1947. A six-month strike in 1954-55 had less success, although at least four bridges were burned along the railroad. During early 1955, the workers returned to their jobs without a new agreement.

By the mid-1940s, the Dierks Lumber & Coal Company was controlled by three Dierks cousins, Herbert, son of Hans Dierks; Frederick, son of Herman Dierks; and DeVere, son of Peter Dierks. They held numerous titles with the lumber company, railroads, and other businesses. In late 1946, Herbert, serving as company president, passed away and it took several years for new titles to be assigned.

In 1954, the company was reorganized again, becoming Dierks Forests, Inc. This new company lasted only 15 years before Weyerhaeuser acquired all of the Dierks holdings during September 1969. At the time, the nearly 2 million acres of timberland transferred was the largest such transaction in the history of the timber business. Production in the area increased with the completion of the pulpmill at Valliant in 1971. However, at about the same time, the last of the log trains made their final journey back from the woods. Trucks began to handle the delivery of raw materials to the mills, especially since it had been determined that it required at least four thousand board feet of timber per acre to log profitably by railroad, but only five hundred board feet to log by truck.

Since then, several mills have been closed while others have been modernized, and the railroads were sold to the Patriot Rail Company in late 2010. While many of the efforts of the Dierks family can be found, few direct signs of the organization still clearly exist.

This sign at De Queen, Arkansas, shows the change in ownership of the DeQueen & Eastern, which is now owned by Patriot Rail.

The Dierks Brothers

As previously stated, the Dierks Lumber & Coal Company can trace its history back to German immigrant Peter Henry Dierks (1824-1908), who became a successful farmer and businessman in eastern Iowa, just north of Clinton. He and his wife, Margaretha Dorothea Fauk Dierks, were the parents of Hans (1850–1929), Henry (1860–1895), Herman (1863–1946), and Peter (1867–1906), as well as three daughters, Catherine Dierks Ronna (1854-1894), Anna Dierks Drumm (1856-1942), and Margaret Dorthea Dierks Rixon (1858-1932).

During the early 1880s, the Dierks Brothers Company was founded by brothers Hans, Henry, Herman, and Peter Dierks, and then it became the Dierks Lumber & Coal Company in 1895, the same year that Henry Dierks passed away. Henry, actually Heinrich, was born near Clinton, Iowa, and died of pneumonia near the same place. Heinrich managed a number of the lumber and coal yards for the firm, and lived on the farm of his father.

Peter Dierks was also born near Clinton, Iowa, and was the youngest of the Dierks brothers involved in the lumber business. When the Dierks Lumber & Coal Company was incorporated, he was made general manager of the firm. Peter stayed connected with the Nebraska operations, but when he passed away from typhoid fever on December 12, 1906, he was the secretary-treasurer of the Dierks Lumber & Coal Company, second vice president of the DeQueen & Eastern Railroad Company, and vice president of the Choctaw Lumber Company. His obituary stated that Peter "had become one of the most prominent lumbermen in Nebraska and was recognized as a thorough business man and by his associates was considered one of the best authorities on any question pertaining to the lumber business."

The deaths of Henry and Peter left just Hans and Herman, the two brothers most associated with the Dierks Lumber & Coal Company. When the company was incorporated in 1895, Hans was made president while Herman was secretary and treasurer, and soon vice president. The two brothers typically swapped titles at different firms owned by the family. For example, in 1925, Herman Dierks was shown as being the president of the Texas, Oklahoma & Eastern, while Hans Dierks was the vice president. At the same time, Hans Dierks was the president and Herman Dierks was the vice president of the DeQueen & Eastern.

Hans Dierks was born in Germany on March 11, 1850, and came to the United States when his mother and father moved here in 1852. He married and moved to western Iowa during the 1870s. Being the eldest brother, he was generally the leader in the family businesses, helping to organize a series of firms over the next several decades. Many reports stated that the capital stock of the various firms were owned by Hans Dierks and other members of the Dierks family. He based his operations out of Kansas City, directing the sales and investment efforts, as well as many of the legal concerns of the various firms. He died at his home on November 11, 1929, reportedly from a severe case of bronchial asthma.

In 1902, Herman Dierks moved to De Queen to manage the sawmill and logging operations, and also to buy more timberland. Herman, who became the brother most associated with the Arkansas operations, was the couple's sixth child and the last to die. Herman was born near Clinton, Iowa, and headed up the family's operations in Lincoln, Nebraska, before moving to Arkansas and Indian Territory. During the 1910s, he held the title of vice president and general manager of the Dierks Lumber & Coal Company, and then became president during the late 1920s. Herman died of a heart seizure while in Pasadena, California, on April 3, 1946.

By the 1920s, the children of Hans, Herman and Peter were involved with managing different parts of the company. Hans' two sons were involved with all parts of the organization. Herbert looked after the sawmills while Harry managed the company's finances and the Nebraska lumber yards. Herman's son Fred followed his father and got into timber buying and logging management. Peter's son DeVere (or Devere) was in charge of lumber sales and marketing.

The children, and even the grandchildren, of the Dierks brothers remained in the company's leadership until the company was sold to Weyerhaeuser in 1969. Comments by some of the family indicated that it was time to sell since the stock was in the hands of hundreds of family members across the country, many having no association with the company's operations.

Peter Dierks Joers was the last Chairman of the Board of Directors for Dierks Forests, Inc. He was born in 1919 to William H. Joers and Catherine (Dierks) Joers, making him the great-grandson of German immigrant Peter Henry Dierks. Unlike much of the family, he grew up in New York City, and then attended the U.S. Naval Academy (Class of 1942). He fought across the Pacific and then became vice president of Dierks in 1946, becoming a business leader in Hot Springs, Arkansas, where he was buried in Greenwood Cemetery in 2006.

A History of the
DeQueen & Eastern Railroad Company

One of the first reports about the DeQueen & Eastern Railroad can be found in the September 21, 1900, issue of the *Arkansas Gazette*. A news item reported:

> *A charter was granted to the DeQueen and Eastern Railroad company at the meeting of the state board of railroad incorporators held yesterday. The road will commence at DeQueen and then run in a north-westerly direction through Sevier, Howard, and Pike Counties, a distance of forty miles to Murfreesboro in Pike County, at which place the road will connect with the Arkansas and Southern from Pike county. The capital stock is $280,000. The incorporators are: Hans Dierks, G. L. Turner, of Kansas City; Herman Dierks, Peter Dierks, of Lincoln, Neb.; Harry Large, W. A. Prater, Herbert Dierks of De Queen; Travis Pope of Center Point; M. F. Allen of Holcomb and Smithson T. Watkins of Cornith, Ark.*

One issue with the report was that there was no "Arkansas and Southern," instead there were some promoted plans for an extension of the Arkansas Southwestern to Murfreesboro. The second issue was that the first track built and operated by the DeQueen & Eastern was a two-mile line that connected the De Queen sawmill with Kansas City Southern, immediately to the west. A final issue was that Murfreesboro was to the northeast, not the northwest. A later report by the Arkansas Corporation Commission stated that the DeQueen & Eastern Railroad was incorporated in Arkansas on September 22, 1900.

Many reports stated that the new railroad was backed by the Dierks Lumber & Coal Company. Evidence of this was an advertisement in the October 13, 1900, issue of *American Lumberman*. It announced that the Dierks Lumber & Coal Company of Lincoln, Nebraska, wanted to buy new or second hand steel rails, about 45 pounds or heavier, for four miles of track, delivered at De Queen, Arkansas.

Despite the control of the railroad by Dierks Lumber & Coal, the first list of railroad operating officials found only one member of the family listed. These first officers of the DeQueen & Eastern Railroad were "Wylie A. Prater, General Manager; Herbert Dierks, Secretary and Treasurer; Harry J. Large, General Passenger and Ticket Agent, also Depot Agent and Auditor; E. B. Ward, Purchasing Agent; W. E. Fields, Roadmaster; C. P. Brown, Construction Superintendent; W. G. Frye, Shop Superintendent; Judge G. A. Vaughn, Civil Engineer; Edward S. Byington, Surveyor; H. Sylvas, Brakeman; and W. S. Frey, Conductor and Trainmaster." By 1904, *Poor's Manual of Railroads* showed that Hans Dierks was president; Herman Dierks was Vice President and General Manager; Peter Dierks was Second Vice President; and Harry J. Large was Auditor, Assistant Secretary and Treasurer.

An interesting detail about the railroad is the spelling of De Queen. While the community has a space between the two parts of the name (De Queen), the railroad does not (DeQueen). You can often find the name of the railroad spelled either way, but internal documents had it spelled DeQueen & Eastern from the start.

The first part of the new railroad came about because when Dierks purchased the Williamson Brothers sawmill, it included a few miles of logging railroad to the east of De Queen. A short piece of track was quickly built that connected with the Kansas City Southern so that lumber could be shipped out easily to other markets, especially to the various lumber yards around Kansas City that were owned by the Dierks brothers. By late 1901, construction was underway to Lockesburg, about a dozen miles to the east. The *De Queen Bee* newspaper reported that the first boxcar for the DeQueen & Eastern's freight business arrived the week of April 18, 1902, and passenger service began by mid-June of 1902. By October, the railroad had been extended another six miles eastward to a location where Dierks planned to build a store, hotel and warehouse. Various rumors at the time had the railroad heading on east to Center Point, and then on to Hot Springs, Arkansas. There was also talk that a line would be built to the southwest from De Queen all the way to Paris, Texas.

Surveys were being made for new railroad construction by the summer of 1904. Reports cited various destinations such as Provo, Murfreesboro, and Hot Springs, all in Arkansas. By late summer of 1905, the railroad had reached the Saline River, and more work was waiting on the completion of the bridge. At the same time, the railroad was expanding its fleet of railcars. The August 4, 1905, issue of *The Railway Age* reported that the DeQueen & Eastern had "ordered 18 logging flat cars from the American Car & Foundry Company."

While the DeQueen & Eastern Railroad Company was incorporated September 22, 1900, records show that the railway officially became the DeQueen & Eastern on June 30, 1905. This issue came about because the 19 miles of road between De Queen and Provo were actually constructed by the Dierks Lumber & Coal Company. In 1905, the property was transferred to the railroad and Dierks Lumber maintained essentially full ownership of the railroad company. A report entitled "Railroad Building in Arkansas 1904-1905" by the Arkansas Railroad Commission stated that the DeQueen & Eastern was planning to build 100 miles of track from Provo northeast to Hot Springs, and that grading on 25 miles was already underway.

The first construction by the railroad took place in 1906 when the line was extended eight more miles to Dierks. The Interstate Commerce Commission also noted that "the carrier acquired various log-spur tracks which served the industries of the Dierks Lumber & Coal Company. These spur tracks, which were often removed and relocated, were abandoned in 1909, and the rail and track fastenings therein were sold to the Dierks Lumber & Coal Company in 1916." Between the various tracks east and west of De Queen, the railroad owned and used "33.430 miles of all tracks," Over these lines, the "industrial railroad" handled "43,000 tons of freight, of which 24,707 tons represented products of forests, most of which was received from the Dierks Lumber & Coal Company, which is controlled by Hans Dierks and other members of the Dierks family, who also control the railroad." The tracks arrived at Dierks in 1906, and twice-daily mixed train service began between De Queen and Dierks. Reports from the time stated that each train operated with two coaches.

The June 25, 1909, issue of the *De Queen Bee* was what it called its Industrial Edition, and it covered the farming and businesses in the region. Several pages were dedicated to the Dierks Lumber & Coal Company and the railroads that it owned. The newspaper provided a great deal of information about how the DeQueen & Eastern was operating and what it was hauling. It described the terminal at De Queen as follows.

> *The terminal facilities at De Queen comprise the general offices, the repair shops, a car shed (60'x132'), a casting yard, a supply house (24'x160') and two and a half miles of terminal trackage. The terminal*

trackage includes a passing track, two shop tracks, a coach track, two RIP tracks, three lumber loading tracks, a storage track for 55 cars, a wye and a transfer track for connection with the K.C.S. railway.

The newspaper also described the freight being moved over the railroad. It listed inbound freight as brick, cement, coal, commercial fertilizers, ice, machinery, salt, sugar, structural steel for county bridges and wagons for farm and logging purposes. The outbound freight showed that the De Queen & Eastern was more than just a logging line. It stated that the railroad handed large volumes of freight off to the Kansas City Southern, consisting of lumber, shingles, staves, crossties, logs, cattle, hogs, sheep, cotton, cotton seed, peaches, potatoes, and radishes. The railroad moved 900-1200 cars of logs and 175 to 225 carloads of lumber a month. It also handled 5-6000 bales of cotton annually, with large volumes of eggs and poultry moving from Locksburg, Provo and Dierks.

In 1910, the DeQueen & Eastern Railroad was investigated as part of the Tap Line Case hearings conducted by the Interstate Commerce Commission (ICC). These hearings evaluated a number of railroads owned by logging companies called "Tap Lines." These lines were essentially industrial railroads serving only their owners, but were established as common carriers to obtain a share of the shipment rate revenue. Many of the lines were found to not be common carriers, and they lost their ability to charge a part of the rate for their services. The ICC hearing determined that the DeQueen & Eastern was a railroad and should receive an appropriate share of the rates quoted by Kansas City Southern. The hearing report contained a number of details that explain the railroad's operations at the time.

As described on the record, the tap line consists of about 27 miles of main track connecting with the Kansas City Southern at De Queen, Ark., extending southeasterly to a point known as Locksburg, and thence northeasterly to its terminus at Dierks. There are also about 15 miles of logging spurs and sidings, and the tap line has steel sufficient for about 30 miles of logging spurs. The tap line claims to have four station buildings along its line, costing about $1,000 each, with a building used as its general office at De Queen. It also has track scales for weighing carload shipments and shops for repairing its equipment. There are 5 locomotives, 3 box cars, 74 flat cars, and 20 other cars, and in addition 2 log loaders. The tap line has 5 station agents, 1 train crew, and a number of track and shop men. It is said that none of its employees work for the lumber company. But the salaries paid by the tap line to its officials, who are also officials of the lumber company, aggregate $650 per month.

For the year ending June 30, 1910, the DeQueen & Eastern reported $54,379.51 in revenue, and $59,049.12 in operating expenses and depreciation. The revenues certainly showed that the railroad was built to haul freight and consisted of:

$46,603.76	freight
$5,303.58	passenger
$977.12	express
$685.31	miscellaneous
$670.53	mail
$139.21	excess baggage

More rail activity took place on October 19, 1910, when the Texas, Oklahoma & Eastern Railroad (TO&E) was incorporated to connect the new Bismark mill and timber to the Arkansas & Choctaw (later Frisco) at Valliant, Oklahoma. This new company didn't immediately impact De Queen. However, when another mill was built in Broken Bow, Oklahoma, the tracks were extended eastward by 1912. With the need to interchange timber and other supplies between the various mills, the two rail lines were extended toward each other over the next decade.

Clearing for what was called the Main Line Extension (Broken Bow to De Queen – MLE in many reports) began on June 1, 1916. This project led to a number of changes and improvements along the entire rail system. On February 23, 1917, the *De Queen Bee* reported that the "general headquarters of the Texas, Oklahoma & Eastern and De-Queen & Eastern railroads have been moved from Broken Bow, Okla, to this city, and now occupy the second floor of the Dierks building at the corner of De Queen avenue and Fourth street." At least three management and office positions moved to De Queen with the change. As part of the move, a telephone line was installed that connected Broken Bow with the general offices in De Queen, and eventually to Dierks to connect all of the offices along the railroad. By August 1923, the *Railway Signal Engineer* magazine reported that the DeQueen & Eastern had 36 miles of telephone, and the Texas, Oklahoma & Eastern had 40 miles of telephone, used in transmitting train orders. No telegraph was used by the two railroads.

On January 5, 1921, the two lines were officially connected at West Line, an otherwise unidentified location near the Arkansas-Oklahoma border. Reportedly, the location was chosen to keep each property operating only in one state, eliminating some regulation and government reporting. As the new route was being completed, the railroad began to spread gravel on the track. Obtained from a series of pits along the Cossatot River east of De Queen, the plan stated in a December 28, 1920, report was to use steam locomotive #375 on the gravel trains, using two sets of rented gravel cars. This would allow one set to be loaded while one set was being distributed. By Fall 1921, more than 300 cars of gravel had been hauled and spread between miles 31 and 48 (Mountain Fork River and De Queen).

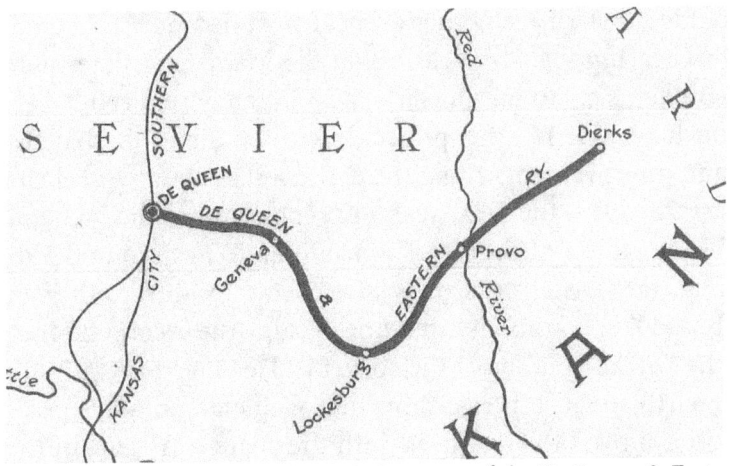

This Interstate Commerce Commission map of the DeQueen & Eastern was produced in 1918 by the Bureau of Valuation.

Despite many reports stating that the line was completed at the state line, the railroad reported that the last spike was driven at 4:23 p.m. on January 5, 1921, not far west of the KCS Crossing at De Queen. At the time, Dierks and their various subsidiaries were operating 77 miles of mainline and more than 150 miles of logging lines. During this entire time, the DQ&E had a controlling interest in the TO&E.

Much of the initial construction of the railroad was conducted using horses, as was much of the original logging. However, machinery soon became involved as the company looked for efficiencies and ways to speed up the work. The construction of both railroads took place with John Cleveland Leeper as Chief Engineer. Records showed that J. C. Leeper had offices at the headquarters of both railroads – De Queen and Broken Bow. Leeper had a long history of railroad construction and maintenance, including the DeQueen & Eastern (1905); Kansas City Southern (1906-1907); Missouri & North Arkansas (1907-1908); Gulf, Mobile & Northern (1908-1909); Kansas City Southern (1909-1910); Stone & Webster Engineering building the Galveston-Houston Electric Railway and the Rio Grande Valley Traction Company (1910-1913); and then back to the DeQueen & Eastern. He is credited with surveying "the optimum route through the rolling hill country of western Sevier County" to connect the two railroads in January 1921. He lived in De Queen the rest of his life and was buried in the local Redman Cemetery in 1965.

This stone marks the burial place of John Cleveland Leeper in Redmen Cemetery at De Queen, Arkansas. J. C. Leeper was the chief railroad engineer for Dierks, and was responsible for much of the construction of the DeQueen & Eastern and Texas, Oklahoma & Eastern.

Another Leeper also had a role with the railroad. Fred J. Leeper was known as the land man, and he bought the right-of-way for the railroad. In 1914, Fred was the Emigrant Agent for the DeQueen & Eastern, based at De Queen. Frederick Jackson "Fred" Leeper was active in De

Queen, and was often shown to be a real estate investor and salesman. In 1918, Fred Leeper was elected alderman of De Queen. He later moved to Hot Springs, Arkansas. Other family members also played roles in developing De Queen, and the name is still common in the community.

Once built, much of the history of the DeQueen & Eastern consists of little more than daily trains operating on a regular schedule to move products for the Dierks Lumber & Coal Company. While spur tracks were built and retired, the mainline was built and few changes took place. However, during the mid-1920s, the two railroads were being investigated by the Interstate Commerce Commission (ICC) as part of its plan to create a few large national railroads, something started during the federal control of the railroad industry during World War I. In 1929, the ICC released its Consolidation Plan, a proposed merger plan to create 21 regional rail systems. As stated by the ICC:

The plan provides for two New England systems, exclusive of the Canadian mileage, each having lines into New York; five eastern systems, one of which, the Wabash, would extend west to Kansas City and south to Florida and another of which, the Baltimore & Ohio, also would be extended to Kansas City by the addition of the Alton; three southern systems, each with access to Chicago, nine western systems, one of which the Chicago and North Western, would also extend south to the Gulf; and the two Canadian systems of the Canadian Pacific and Canadian National.

As a part of this consolidation plan, DQ&E/TO&E would have been part of System No. 19, known as the Rock Island-Frisco system. However, the Kansas City Southern was to be part of the Union Pacific system, creating some conflict in potential freight movements for the Dierks Lumber & Coal Company. By the time the ICC announced its plan, several mergers were underway, many very different from what were being proposed. Many other railroads remained independent, including the DeQueen & Eastern Railroad.

In 1954, the ownership of the two railroads was transferred to the new Dierks Forests organization. The DQ&E line was extended further to the east at Perkins and opened on January 10, 1957. This new line was built to provide an eastern outlet to get raw materials to a new kraft paper mill at Pine Bluff, Arkansas. This mill was built by Dierks, and using the Perkins connection with Missouri Pacific meant that only one other railroad would have to be used to move woodchips and other products to Pine Bluff, as opposed to at least two if the materials were handed off to Kansas City Southern at De Queen, or the Frisco at Valliant. In September 1969, the entire package of mills, timber and railroads was sold to Weyerhaeuser Company for $192,000,000.

In 1979, a report about the railroad listed the products being shipped on the railroad. At Valliant was brown paper for corrugated cardboard. Wright City produced wood chips, lumber, plywood and railroad ties. The mill at Craig produced insulated board, particle board, and siding. The treatment plant west of De Queen shipped treated fence posts and poles. The complex at Dierks produced a number of products, and the railroad hauled lumber, plywood, wood chips, hardwood planks, and charcoal. Finally, gypsum board was moved from Briar.

Since then, there have been a number of changes in the mills and shippers along the railroad, and Weyerhaeuser sold the rail lines to Patriot Rail on December 30, 2010, creating the DeQueen and Eastern Railroad, LLC. The purchase of the DeQueen & Eastern and the Texas, Oklahoma & Eastern by Patriot Rail was part of a larger purchase of a number of railroads owned by Weyerhaeuser. This included the Columbia & Cowlitz Railway and the Weyerhaeuser Woods Railroad in Washington, as well as the Golden Triangle Railroad and the Mississippi & Skuna Valley Railroad in Mississippi. All totaled, the purchase involved six railroads in four states, 160 track miles that handled about 60,000 rail carloads a year, and "28 locomotives, over 300 owned railcars and 2500 leased ones, plus some road vehicles, real estate and office buildings, track maintenance equipment, locomotive shops, rail car repair shops, a wheel shop, and rail yards."

On March 4, 2011, the Surface Transportation Board granted authority to the new DeQueen & Eastern Railroad to "lease and operate 40 miles of railroad owned by the Texas, Oklahoma & Eastern Railroad." With this, the railroad is operated along with its affiliate, the Texas, Oklahoma and Eastern Railroad, as a single combined railroad with 91 miles of track.

Today the DeQueen & Eastern/Texas, Oklahoma & Eastern is about as modern as a small railroad can be. They are fully capable of repairing their own equipment and track. They have added new ties and welded rail to handle heavier loads of pulpboard, wood chips, corn, stone, paper, soybeans and chemicals. Several modern bridges have been installed to handle heavier loads. As stated by its owners, the "DQE interchanges with BNSF via the Kiamichi Railroad at Valliant, Oklahoma; the Kansas City Southern in De Queen, Arkansas; and the UP at Perkins, Arkansas." The firm "owns a car repair facility, a fully equipped wheel shop and a locomotive repair shop in De Queen, Arkansas. Both facilities are equipped with overhead cranes and the locomotive shop is also equipped with a pit and traction motor turntable. There is a maintenance of way building located in De Queen that has an equipment repair shop with overhead crane, pit, wash and service area. In Valliant,

Oklahoma, there is a maintenance of way equipment repair facility with a wash area and storage, and an open car repair shed with two tracks under roof with capacity for 4 cars and a ready track that will hold 6 cars."

Wood chips are still a major commodity moved by the DeQueen & Eastern, as shown by this train at De Queen in 2023.

The 1910 Tap Line Case Hearing

The investigation into the railroad by the Interstate Commerce Commission (ICC), part of the Tap Line Case, was previously mentioned. This series of hearings into a large number of small railroads, many essentially logging railroads operating for the benefit of their owners, lasted over several years and resulted in the ICC declaring that many of the freight rates charged, or the division share of the rates charged, were illegal because the Tap Lines were not real railroads but simply industrial rail operations. However, some of these decisions were overturned by the U.S. Supreme Court and broader definitions of a railroad were created by the ICC to comply with the rulings.

As a part of the Tap Line case investigations, the railroads participated in hearings where they were asked questions and they could provide information about their operations in an attempt to justify receiving a share of the freight rates involved with moving products across their lines. The hearing for the DeQueen & Eastern took place at New Orleans, Louisiana, on December 17, 1910, after what was apparently a ten-day delay where representatives of the railroad simply sat and waited for their opportunity to speak. Based upon the minutes of the meeting, the hearing was not always friendly, with the representative of the ICC stopping the testimony a number of times in an effort to speed up the hearing, often simply saying that the speaker was wasting their time.

A major part of the hearing was spent investigating the value of the DeQueen & Eastern Railroad and whether it deserved the revenue that it received from moving logs to the mills, and the finished lumber to Kansas City Southern (KCS) at De Queen. At the time, the railroad had a contract with Dierks Lumber & Coal that provided that "all the logs hauled up to the mill shall be manufactured into lumber by the Dierks Lumber Company, and be shipped out to market over the lines of the Kansas City Southern from the town of De Queen." The contract set a $6.00 charge per car for the hauling of the logs on the spur tracks to the DeQueen & Eastern mainline, and also a charge of $1.25 for loading logs on single-length cars, and $2.50 for longer cars that could hold two lengths of logs. The mainline rates used were joint milling in-transit rates that included the movement of the logs to the mill, and then the lumber to markets using the Kansas City Southern. As a part of this rate, the DeQueen & Eastern received a division of the KCS rate that equaled 2 to 6 cents per hundredweight (100 pounds). It was clearly stated that the same rates applied to Dierks and any other timber company on the line. At the time, 53.9% of earnings came from Dierks forest products, 21.6% of earnings came from the forest products of other companies, and 24.5% of earnings came from non-forest product shipments.

The Interstate Commerce Commission determined that the railroad served 6 sawmills and 5 cotton gins, and "two or three regular loading stock yards." Besides lumber products, the railroad was paid to haul cotton, hay, salt, cotton seed, livestock, and flour. The railroad owned 5 locomotives (it had 6 but one had recently burned), 74 flat cars, 3 box cars, 2 tank cars, 1 gondola, 2 log loaders, a combined ditcher and pile driver, 2 passenger cars, and 15 boarding cars used as housing by workers.

The railroad had a number of spur tracks, most used for timber loading. It was stated that these log spurs were "laid according to the lay of the land" and that they were no "closer than three miles and none of them are five miles apart." It was also noted that the railroad was unique in that it had a number of "permanent" structures such as two large steel bridges (200 feet and 150 feet) that were set on concrete filled cylinders for piers, or timber piles. Many of the details about specific station locations are cited in this book's route guide chapter.

The hearing and case apparently did not go well for the DeQueen & Eastern as the ICC ruled that no division of the KCS rate should be allowed for the De Queen mill. Instead, the railroad should simply receive $1.50 per carload for lumber moved between the De Queen sawmill and the Kansas City Southern. However, by this time, the mill was closed and lumber was being cut elsewhere, and apparently the rate division was fine for these longer moves.

The fact that the ICC seemed to declare the DeQueen & Eastern to be a real railroad, and not simply a tap line, had significant benefits in the future as the company was allowed to create rates for various products, but it was forced to comply with both Arkansas and federal regulations and practices. Another federal government organization, the Railroad Retirement Board, has reported that the DeQueen & Eastern Railroad became covered by the program starting on September 22, 1900.

A Part of a Greater Plan?

Over the years, there were many announced plans to extend the DeQueen & Eastern, many made by those outside the company and a few by those within. Hot Springs always seemed to be a goal of the railroad. However, none of these plans matched those promoted in 1907 and 1911. These plans started with G. H. Cravens, the former chief engineer of the Memphis, Paris & Gulf Railway, later the Memphis, Dallas & Gulf Railroad (M.D.&G.). This company had started in 1906 as the Memphis, Paris & Gulf, and had plans to build across Arkansas to reach Memphis, Tennessee The plan was to acquire a number of logging railroads and to connect them into a much larger mainline railroad. In 1910, the Nashville Lumber Company merged with the Grayson-McLeod Lumber Company, and the railroad became the Memphis, Dallas & Gulf Railroad.

The January 11, 1907, issue of *The Railway Age* carried news about plans to extend the DeQueen & Eastern. "G. H. Cravens, chief engineer, De Queen, Ark., reports that the extension of this road from Provo to Dierks, Ark., 8 miles, has been completed and that it is proposed to build from Dierks to Hot Springs, Ark., 100 miles, and also from De Queen to Paris, Tex."

G. H. Cravens continued this dream, looking even farther afield. His plan was to connect the DeQueen & Eastern with Little Rock, then build to the southwest through Idabel, Oklahoma, and Clarksville, Texas, to reach Dallas. From Little Rock, the railroad would build northward to

St. Louis. Among the railroads to be included in the plan were the DeQueen & Eastern; the Little Rock, Maumelle & Western; the Caddo & Choctaw; and A. L. Clark's lumber railroad. By February, De Queen, Little Rock, and other communities along the proposed route had decided to aid Cravens in promoting the construction of the railroad.

During one of these meetings, Cravens made an interesting statement. He commented that he was working out "legislative and other problems" with the plan. Financing was certainly an issue, as it had been with the very similar plan announced when Cravens was working for the Memphis, Dallas & Gulf. By late April of 1911, news about Cravens' project disappeared.

In the June 30, 1911, issue of the *De Queen Bee*, there were again multiple articles about the DeQueen & Eastern being expanded to Hot Springs. Herman Dierks was quoted several times as stating that the line would be built. The newspaper quoted him as saying that: "We will build our line to Hot Springs, and without bonus, excepting depot grounds and right-of-way, to be given by Hot Springs people, regardless of the M.D.&G. building into that city. We first want to make surveys, which will require a few months, and then we will put the proposition up to them. The M.D.&G. is trying to head us off by buying these log roads, but they will find out D.&E. will run into Hot Springs just the same." A letter received by the newspaper from Herman Dierks a few days later added to the details.

I also understand that the M.D.&G. has an option to buy a couple of log lines over which to reach Hot Springs. These log lines are in a somewhat similar direction to the route we are figuring on. But we believe a new road of better alignment than these log lines, with a good grade line, built up to standard railroad specifications, would make a much more satisfactory

> *road. As you know most of these log spurs are built in an up and down way and are generally very crooked. So we feel that the best thing to do is to build a new line throughout, and I believe that we can get a grade line not to exceed a five-tenths grade, and just as soon as our engineers complete our line west of De Queen, known as the Texas, Oklahoma & Eastern, we are going to make a complete survey to Hot Springs. I wish further to state that we have no bond issue or any indebtedness whatever on the DeQueen & Eastern or the Texas, Oklahoma & Eastern, so that in a financial way we ought to be able to carry out our program as heretofore outlined. The main thing that we are after is to make a good railroad and a low freight line out of it, and we will eventually connect with the northern Texas lines and southern lines, so that it will be an elegant passenger line to Hot Springs, as well as a freight line.*

By this time, Matt Allen, Superintendent of the De-Queen & Eastern, had already met with officers of the Hot Springs Commercial League with the proposal for a right-of-way and depot property. There was also speculation that the company would build on to Little Rock and even St. Louis, and from Valliant to Dallas. While these grand plans were never achieved, other smaller plans were promoted for years. One of these was the construction of the Texas, Oklahoma & Eastern Railroad.

The Texas, Oklahoma & Eastern Railroad Company

The Texas, Oklahoma & Eastern forms the western half of the DeQueen & Eastern rail system. The Texas, Oklahoma & Eastern Railroad Company was incorporated in Oklahoma on October 21, 1910. An initial report about the railroad stated that it was to be built between Valliant and Idabel, Oklahoma. However, it was quickly announced that the charter was to cover "the line of road already in operation from Valliant to a point near Lukfata. The road has been operating as a part of the Choctaw Lumber Co., and is spoken of as the western extension of the DeQueen & Eastern."

Much of the news about its earliest years generally just noted it as a project of Dierks Lumber & Coal, the Choctaw Lumber Company, or the DeQueen & Eastern Railroad. A report in the May 5, 1911, issue of the *Railway Age Gazette* stated that the railroad "has work underway on four miles and track already finished on 19 miles. The plans call for building from Valliant, Okla., through McCurtain county, east through a timber section, via Bismarck, to Mountain Fork river, 30 miles, and it is understood the line will eventually be extended into Arkansas." Operations began in June 1911.

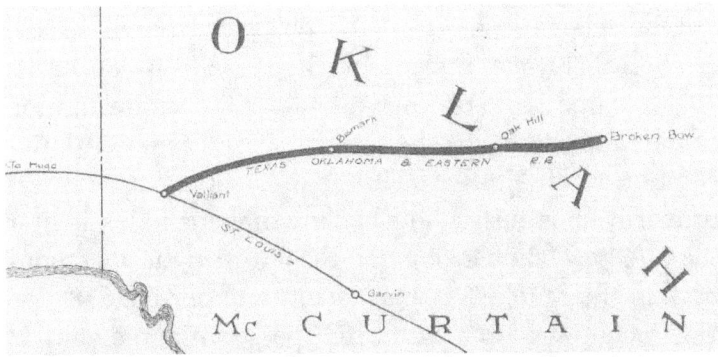

In a 1918 valuation report, the Interstate Commerce Commission produced this map for the Texas, Oklahoma & Eastern. At the time, the railroad only connected Valliant with Broken Bow.

A 1926 Interstate Commerce Commission valuation report about the TO&E stated that in 1918, the railroad connected Valliant and Broken Bow, "a distance of 24.070

miles. The carrier also owns 7.461 miles of yard tracks and sidings." The report had the interesting statement that the "bridge steel and a portion of the rails and fastenings in the track are leased from the St. Louis-San Francisco Railway Company." This was apparently 50 to 65-pound relay rail that was used on yard tracks and sidings. The ICC also stated that the DeQueen & Eastern Railroad Company owned "over 99 per cent of its outstanding capital stock." (*Poor's Manual of Railroads* stated that in 1918 the DeQueen & Eastern owned $199,300 of the $200,000 of capital stock of the Texas, Oklahoma & Eastern Railroad Company. One share, valued at $100 each, was owned by each company director – Hans Dierks, Herman Dierks, Frederick Dierks, Harry L. Dierks, J. S. Kirkpatrick, C. E. Baxter, and H. M. Kirkpatrick.) The ICC report also stated that the track from Valliant to Broken Bow was "constructed for the carrier by the Choctaw Lumber Company during the period 1910 and 1911." At the time, the Choctaw Lumber Company was affiliated with the Dierks Lumber & Coal Company.

One delay in completing the Texas, Oklahoma & Eastern was that it was under federal control from January 1, 1918, to June 25, 1918. This was part of the nationalization of the rail industry by the United States Railroad Administration (USRA). The USRA found that the TO&E was primarily an industrial line hauling timber and lumber for the Choctaw Lumber Company, so it turned the operations back to the railroad's management on June 26, 1918. The USRA continued to monitor the operations of the railroad until February 29, 1920. An interesting finding after World War I was that the TO&E had actually made too much money to have the federal government reimburse it for the takeover in 1918.

The line was slowly built eastward as mills and logging sites were added, and the railroad constructed 15.66 miles of railroad from Broken Bow to the Arkansas state line in

1921. On January 3, 1921, the Texas, Oklahoma & Eastern filed a request with the Interstate Commerce Commission for a certificate of public convenience to operate the entire railroad. In 1931, the Interstate Commerce Commission reported that the railroad owned and operated 39.74 miles of track, and that it was an operating subsidiary of Dierks Lumber & Coal Company.

The DeQueen & Eastern was a relatively late user of cabooses, as shown by this 1989 photo of TOE caboose #86 following a freight train near De Queen, Arkansas.

On November 1, 2010, the Surface Transportation Board gave Patriot Rail's Texas, Oklahoma & Eastern Railroad, LLC, authority to acquire and operate the Texas, Oklahoma & Eastern Railroad. A few months later, the DeQueen & Eastern Railroad, LLC was given authority to lease and operate the new TO&E. For most people, there is no difference between the two railroads and the locomotives of each line can be found anywhere on the almost 90-mile operation.

The railroad moves more than 30,000 carloads a year, with 31,194 in 2015, and 31,286 in 2016. These movements included pulpboard, paper, corn, stone, and wood chips. Today, the DeQueen & Eastern, and its sister company, the Texas, Oklahoma & Eastern, operate an 86-mile line between Perkins, Arkansas, and Valliant, Oklahoma, under the ownership of Patriot Rail. These lines still serve area industries such as wood, paper, and poultry. Thousands of area residents depend on the railroad to move the products they produce or use.

A Short History of the Line's Passenger Service

Many years ago, passenger service on these lines provided an essential service to the many small, isolated communities in this area, and often to get the loggers to their work sites. Things were never fancy. Several early pictures show the typical wooden coaches behind one of the DQ&E 4-6-0 or 2-6-2 steam locomotives. Note that almost every single steam locomotive acquired by the company was new; second hand locomotives would seldom do for this prosperous operation. The same applied to the first passenger cars used on the railroad.

During May 1902, the *De Queen Bee* newspaper reported that the "first passenger coach arrived via KCS, built by Jackson & Sharp Company of Wilmington, Delaware." The Jackson & Sharp Company was a railroad car manufacturer and shipbuilder, founded in 1863, leased to American Car & Foundry (ACF) in 1901, and sold to ACF in 1911. The company operated their Delaware Car Works, located in Wilmington, Delaware, and produced as many as 400 passenger cars per year. The firm was known for its decorative wooden passenger cars, but also for producing passenger cars for narrow-gauge and shortline railroads. More passenger cars arrived, and on March 2, 1903, the DeQueen & Eastern began carrying mail between De Queen and Locksburg.

The 1910 passenger service was obviously designed for on-line needs as it didn't connect with any KCS train without at least a several hour wait in De Queen. Train No. 1

would depart De Queen eastbound at 9:30am daily except Sunday. It would arrive at Dierks at 11:45am. At 1:05pm, the train would turn as train No. 2, arriving back at De Queen at 3:15pm. About this time, the railroad also operated a number of special trains for picnics, Fourth of July celebrations, and church gatherings.

958
DE QUEEN & EASTERN RAILROAD.

HANS DIERKS, President,   Kansas City, Mo.
HERMAN DIERKS, Vice-President & Gen. Mgr.,   ”
M. F. ALLEN, General Superintendent,   De Queen, Ark.
JOHN S. KIRKPATRICK, General Counsel,   ”
O. O. RAY, Asst. Treas. and Gen. Freight and Pas. Agt.,   ”
HERBERT DIERKS, Purchasing Agent,   ”
M. G. BOCK, Supt. Motive Power and Trainmaster   ”
(*The G. F. & P. Agt. has charge of accounts.*)
General Offices—De Queen, Ark.

	No. 1	Mls	*November*, 1909.	No. 2		
			LEAVE] [ARRIVE			
	†9 30 A M	0	De Queen[1]	3 15 P M		
	9 45 ”	7	Geneva	2 45 ”		
	10 15 ”	12	Locksburg	2 30 ”		
	10 45 ”	19	Provo	1 55 ”		
	11 45 A M	27	Dierks	†1 05 P M		
			ARRIVE] [LEAVE			

Line under construction 25 miles.
† Daily, except Sunday.   STANDARD—*Central time.*
Connections.—[1] With Kansas City Southern Ry.

This timetable from *The Official Guide of the Railways*, January 1910, page 958, shows the basic passenger schedule from that time. Also note that the railroad was shown to be De Queen & Eastern instead of the more typical DeQueen & Eastern.

On June 14, 1910, the Committee on the Post-Office and Post-Roads of the U.S. House of Representatives held a hearing on the "Mail Pay on Short-Line Railroads." Among the routes examined was Route 147029 over the DeQueen & Eastern Railroad. This hearing looked at the cost of the mail service as well as how the mail was moved from the trains to the post offices. For those who are interested, a rod is equal to 16.5 feet.

Route 147029, De Queen and Eastern Railroad, between De Queen and Dierks Ark., is 27.02 miles long and the service is six days a week. They pay out in cash for messenger service in delivering mail from the station to the post-office as follows: De Queen, 85 rods, $8.33 per month; Locksburg, 12 miles 120 rods, $3 per month; Provo, 19 miles 1 rod, $0 (on account of post-office being in depot building); Dierks, 27.02 miles 70 rods, $5 per month; total, $16.33 per month; the road also charges $10 per month for handling and forwarding mails at each station, making a total charge of $42.33, so that the road actually receives $640.92 per annum for the mail service. The receipts of the road from passengers last year were $5,363.33 and from freight, $93,053.77, and our total receipts, $106,433.81. The operating expenses were $83,757.99 and the taxes $2,153.38, showing a net profit of $20,522.44. The weight of mails we are now actually carrying is 25 per cent greater than in the previous weighing period ending in 1903.

Within a year, passenger trains were also operating on the Texas, Oklahoma & Eastern. Reports from the railroad state that passenger service between Valliant and Broken Bow began on Saturday, July 14, 1911. The train used a "new red passenger coach that had been built in the DeQueen and Eastern Railroad shops at DeQueen, Arkansas." This service was extended eastward as the line was completed towards De Queen.

Because the railroad was built to haul the freight of the Dierks Lumber & Coal Company, the rates were initially low. For the year ending June 30, 1912, the DeQueen & Eastern had $16,090 in freight revenue, and $9319 in passenger revenue. This would probably be the peak of passenger revenue compared with freight revenue. For example, in 1939, freight revenue was $77,461, passenger revenue $713, mail revenue $3991, and express revenue $301.

THE DEQUEEN & EASTERN
Time Table

Effective Monday, February 17, 1913.

	Eastbound	Westbound
	Mix. No. 1	Mix. No. 2
Stations	Dept.	Arrive
De Queen	3 p. m.	11 a. m.
Geneva	3:20 p. m.	10:35 a. m.
Lockesburg	3:50 p. m.	10:10 a. m.
Coulter Spur		F
Provo	4:20 p. m.	9:40 a. m.
Jct. Spur	4:30 p. m. F.	9:25 a. m.
Shrum Springs		F
Dierks	5:00 p. m.	9:10 a. m.

Trains Daily Except Sunday

F. indicates stop flag.

Westbound trains have right over eastbound trains of same or inferior class.

Approved: M. F. Allen, Gen. Supt.
M. G. Bock, Trainmaster.

This February 17, 1913, timetable was published in the *De Queen Bee* newspaper and showed that the passenger service at the time used mixed trains. *De Queen Bee*, De Queen, Ark., February 21, 1913, pg 7. Chronicling America: Historic American Newspapers. Library of Congress. https://chroniclingamerica.loc.gov/lccn/sn89051293/1913-02-21/ed-1

TIME TABLE NO. 16
De Queen & Eastern Railroad Company

(This Time Table Supersedes Previous Numbers)

No. 1. First Class		No. 2. First Class
Mixed leaves daily except Sunday		Mixed arrives daily Except Sunday
Departs	Stations	Arrives
10:00 a. m.	De Queen	4:00 p. m.
10:25 a. m.	(F) Geneva	3:30 p. m.
10:50 a. m.	Lockesburg	3:10 p. m.
11:20 a. m.	Provo	2:40 p. m.
	(F) Junction 21	
	(F) Shrum Springs	
11:50 a. m. Arrives	Dierks	2:10 p. m. Departs
Arrives daily except Sunday		Departs daily except Sunday

East bound trains have right over west bound trains of same or inferior class.
(F) Stop on flag.

DeQueen & Eastern Time Table No. 16 still showed mixed trains handling passengers, and that they operated daily except Sunday. *De Queen Bee*, De Queen, Ark., September 22, 1916. Chronicling America: Historic American Newspapers. Library of Congress. https://chroniclingamerica.loc.gov/lccn/sn89051293/1916-09-22/ed-1/seq-3/

In 1925, the railroad operated a daily except Sunday morning train from De Queen to Dierks and back. The eastbound train departed De Queen at 6:00am as train No. 2, and arrived at Dierks at 7:30am. It returned as train No. 1, leaving Dierks at 8:45am and arriving at De Queen at 10:15am. Between Valliant and De Queen, trains operated daily except Sunday as Nos. 9 and 10, and on Sundays as Nos. 1 and 2. Train No. 9 would leave De Queen at 12:01pm and arrive at Valliant at 3:25pm. It would turn and depart as train No. 10 at 4:35pm, arriving back at De Queen at 8:00pm. The Sunday trains would run quicker due to the lack of local work at the many Dierks company towns and mills.

	2	2	10	Ms	*July 26*, 1925.	9	1	1		
.....	P M	.....	P M	...	(*T. O. & E. R.R.*)	P M	....	P M	...	
.....	3415	.....	†4 35	0	lve.....**Valliant**¹⊙ .arr.	3 25	....	3 15	...	
.....	4 45	.....	5 15	8	...... Wright City ....⊙	2 55	....	2 45	...	
.....	6 00	.....	5 30	15	.........Golden.......⊙	2 10	....	2 10	...	
.....	5 10	.....	5 40	19	.........Oak Hill........	1 55	....	2 00	...	
.....	5 30	.....	6 45	24	......Broken Bow ....⊙	1 40	....	1 50	...	
.....	5 55	.....	7 15	34	.......Eagletown.....⊙	12 50	....	1 10	...	
.....	....	.....	....	..	(*D. Q. & E. R.R.*)	....	....	....	...	
.....	6 10	.....	7 30	41	.......West Line.......	12 30	....	1250	...	
.....	6 40	A M	8 00	50	arr....**De Queen**²⊙ lve.	†12 01	A M	1230	...	
.....	P M	†6 00	P M	50	lve....**De Queen** ...arr.	P M	1015	§P M	...	
.....	....	6 15	.....	56	..... Geneva	.....	9 48	....	...	
.....	....	6 45	.....	61	...... Lockesburg ....⊙	.....	9 35	....	...	
.....	....	7 05	.....	63	.... Provo ....⊙	.....	9 05	....	...	
.....	....	7 30	.....	76	.........**Dierks** ......⊙	.....	†8 45	....	...	
.....	....	A M	.....	..	ARRIVE] [LEAVE	.....	A M	....	...	

(*Texas, Oklahoma & Eastern R.R.—Continued.*)
W. R. LATHAM, Purchasing Agent,   De Queen, Ark.
L. W. HARTSELL, Trainmaster,   "
J. E. DOGGETT, Roadmaster,   "
Dr. W. E. WISDOM, Chief Surgeon,   Broken Bow, Okla.

Right margin note: †Daily, except Sunday; §Sunday only. ⊙ Telephone stations. STANDARD—*Central time.*

Connections.—¹With St. Lo.-San Fran. Ry.   ²With Kan. City So. Ry.

This timetable from *The Official Guide of the Railways*, February 1926, page 1279, shows the much more complex passenger train schedule used in July 1925.

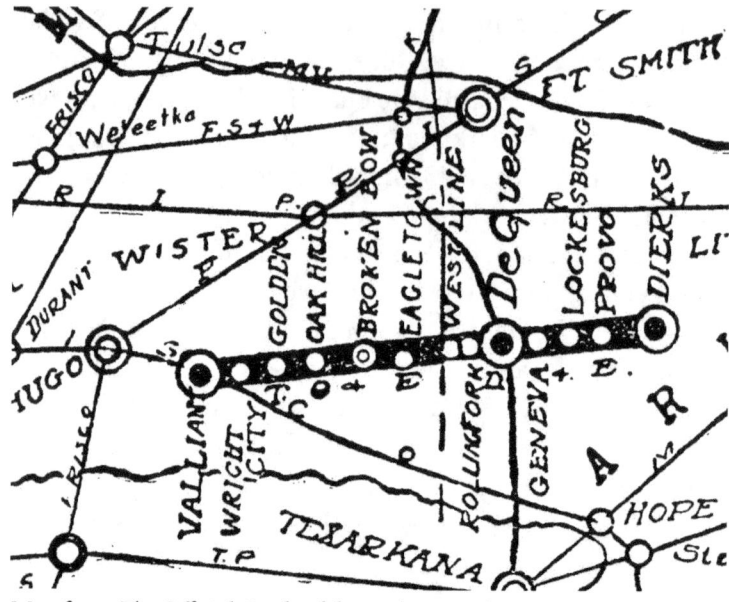

Map from *The Official Guide of the Railways*, February 1926, page 1279.

On May 23, 1926, several newspapers announced that the DeQueen & Eastern began using a 12-passenger Hudson bus that had been rebuilt with flanged railroad wheels. The bus cost less to operate and was more modern in style than the old wooden coaches. The newspapers also stated that the Hudson bus would be used to move mail once approval was received from post office officials.

Dierks was a big fan of the homemade motor, built to save money when compared with using a steam locomotive and full train crew. From the start, the company rebuilt several trucks with rail wheels to move equipment, supplies and personnel to various locations along the logging lines. Several of these used the shells of small buses. One of the first was sporty DQ&E motor bus #5, built using a 1926 Hudson. Two of the most used were TO&E #6 and DQ&E #7. Both reportedly used a bus shell fitted with a 1935 International engine. Each pulled a 4-wheel baggage and express car – very Rio Grande Southern in concept.

In January 1945, the level of service was very similar. Mixed Train No. 9 left De Queen daily except Sunday at 6:35am and headed west to Valliant, arriving there at 10:30am. It turned as Mixed Train No. 10 at noon and arrived back at De Queen at 3:10pm. On Sundays, Train No. 1 used a motor, leaving De Queen at 8:45am and arriving at Valliant at 11:00am. It then left Valliant at 11:20am as Train No. 2, and arrived back at De Queen at 1:25pm. On the east end of the rail system, motor Train No. 6 departed De Queen at 1:00pm daily except Sunday. It then arrived at Dierks at 2:10pm, turned, and left at 3:40pm as Train No. 7. It finished its days at 4:45pm at De Queen.

As roads were built into the area, the private automobile reduced the need for the limited passenger service which the lines provided. By the 1940s, service was reduced to mixed train (handling both freight and passengers) service between Valliant and De Queen and motor service between De Queen and Dierks. These trains only operated Monday through Saturday. Sundays saw only the railcar running between De Queen and Valliant. Mail and passenger service on the DQ&E system ended in 1948. However, reportedly the famous mileage collectors Lucius Beebe and Charles Clegg failed to make the trip in normal fashion several years before that. It seems that the last DQ&E passenger car unexpectedly became a pile of ashes the day before their visit. Check out their comments in the book *Mixed Train Daily.*

Train Operations During the 1970s and 1980s

The 1950s and 1960s saw train operations unhindered by passenger service, but the days of operating steam locomotives ended with the arrival of a series of diesel-electric locomotives. During this time, the loading of logs on temporary spur tracks also ended, with trucks allowing for the use of just a few centralized loading locations.

The two railroads during the 1970s focused primarily on connecting the various mills of the Weyerhaeuser Company. Gone were the many logging trains that had once operated over the mainline, plus all of the motorcars and mixed trains. Three freight trains made roundtrips each day except Sunday, connecting the various mills and yard facilities. A typical day started at 8am as train No. 6 departed De Queen and headed east to Dierks (10:15am) and Perkins (10:40am). At 1:30pm, the freight, now operating as No. 7, would head back west through Dierks (2:00pm), with a scheduled arrival of 3:00pm at De Queen.

On the western part of the railroad, train No. 9 would switch Broken Bow and then depart for Wright City at 10:30am, arriving there at 11:05am. The train would switch the mill at Wright City and then depart (now as train No. 10) at 2:00pm with a scheduled arrival at Broken Bow at 2:30pm. To connect Valliant with De Queen, a night turn operated over the line. Designated as train No. 3, it would leave De Queen at 6:30pm, stopping at Broken Bow (8:00pm) and Wright City (8:45pm) before arriving at North Valliant at 9:05pm. There, traffic was interchanged with the Frisco using the several tracks north of where the diamond is today. The train was scheduled to head back east at 1:30am as No. 4. It had a scheduled time of 2:30am at Broken Bow and then 3:30am at De Queen. In addition, trains were often assigned to Wright City and Dierks to handle local switching at the mills.

The big change during the 1970s was the construction of the large paper board mill at Valliant. The need to switch the mill and to supply it with wood chips often made it the center of the railroad's operations. A presentation by railroad officials in 1982 described the train operations at the time. It was stated that there were three local trains operating five days a week, plus two unit trains operating five days per week. Additionally, there were eight switch crews serving the major mills along the railroad. The busiest operation was at Valliant, where three switch crews provided 24-hour service seven days per week. At Wright City, three switch crews worked five or six days per week. At the east end of the railroad, two switch crews worked five or six days per week at Dierks.

Train Operations During the 1990s

The 1990s may have been the peak of diesel train operations on the DeQueen & Eastern Railroad. It was during this time that the October 1990 issue of *Trains* magazine featured the J. Parker Lamb article "Rails through the Ouachita forests." The article included a good history of the two railroads as well as a look at their current operations.

At the time, almost a dozen trains operated daily on the railroad, handling the various mills and moving wood chips and lumber toward their markets. Several locals operated over the railroad, and a number of Dodgers handled the major terminals of Valliant, Wright City and Dierks. The following is a review of these trains from the early 1990s.

De Queen Day Local – On duty at 10am Sunday through Friday, operated De Queen-Dierks-Valliant-De Queen.

De Queen Night Local – On duty shortly before midnight Sunday through Friday, operated De Queen-Dierks-Valliant-De Queen.

De Queen West Call Local – On duty at 5pm Sunday through Friday, operated De Queen-Craig-De Queen and switched the DQ&E rip track and yard, KCS interchange, pole treatment at Process City, and Tyson feed mill at Craig.

Valliant Dodger #1 (midnight), #2 (8am) and #3 (4pm) – Operated 7 days per week to switch the Valliant mill, handle the Kiamichi interchange, and blocked cars for the locals.

Wright City Dodger #1 (7am) and #2 (5pm) – Operated Monday through Friday to switch the Wright City mill, deliver wood chips to the Valliant mill, and block cars for the locals.

Dierks Dodger #1 (7am) and #2 (5pm) – Operated Monday through Friday to switch the lumber mill at Dierks, work the wallboard plant at Briar, handle the Union Pacific interchange at Perkins, and block cars for the locals.

Dierks Dodger #3 – On duty at 2pm on Sunday only to switch the lumber mill at Dierks, work the wallboard plant at Briar, handle the Union Pacific interchange at Perkins, and block cars for the locals.

This pattern of freight train operations held on through the early 2000s, with the addition of a series of coal trains between De Queen and the Western Farmers Electric Cooperative Hugo Plant near Valliant. However, the closure of the wood treatment plant at Process City and the mill at Wright City, plus the coal business to Western Farmers, greatly reduced the number of trains on the railroad by the 2010s.

The DeQueen & Eastern is not some poor short line operation. This 115 pound-per-yard welded rail dates from 2000 and can be found at the U.S. Highway 278 grade crossing east of Dierks, Arkansas.

Today's Operations

The freight train operations in the 2020s are different from the 1990s. The two large mills at Valliant and Dierks are now the centers of the railroad operations. This traffic is interchanged with three major carriers – BNSF via the Kiamichi Railroad at Valliant, Kansas City Southern (Canadian Pacific Kansas City as of April 14, 2023) at De Queen, and Union Pacific at Perkins. The trains that operate are based upon the needs and schedules of the two large mills and other smaller customers, and the interchange business with the larger railroads.

Two series of local switchers work at the major mills. At Valliant, DeQueen & Eastern trains switch the International Paper (former Weyerhaeuser) mill, plus handle the interchange business and build trains for the movement east to De Queen. These trains operate 24 hours daily, seven days a week and are known as the Valliant Dodger or Switcher. At Dierks, a local handles the new Weyerhaeuser lumber mill, the gypsum mill at Briar, and the interchange business at Perkins. Known as the East Local, it generally goes on duty early in the morning on weekdays.

Connecting these local switchers are several turns operating out of De Queen. A daylight turn, often still known as the Dodger, heads east to Dierks. It first handles local switching at De Queen, and then the interchange business with Kansas City Southern (CPKC). When this is finished, it makes a run to Dierks and then returns, generally on weekdays.

A Valliant Turn, commonly referred to as the Valliant Local, operates from De Queen to Valliant and back, generally running at night. Arriving back at De Queen, it typically leaves many of its freight cars west of the diamond. A few extra trains can sometimes be found operating on the railroad, usually based out of De Queen.

The trains between De Queen and Valliant operate almost exclusively at night. The schedule is generally so reliable that this dog can be found almost every day sleeping on the tracks not far west of Yanubbee Creek.

The railroad historically used timetables and train orders to operate its trains, but then used block limits (Block Register Territory) between the yard limit areas of Valliant, De Queen, Dierks, and Perkins. On August 17, 2017, the railroad replaced the Block Register Territory practice with Track Warrant Control. It soon went back to using blocks. These signs, and those for the various stations protected by yard limit restrictions, can be found all along the railroad. However, during early 2023, the railroad again began to use track warrant control through a contract firm that specializes in dispatching services.

Signs like this mark the ends of each block, once used to provide operating authority for the various trains on the DeQueen & Eastern Railroad.

Signs like this stand along the tracks to mark the start of the various Yard Limits on the railroad.

The Locomotives of the Dierks Railroads

Tracking the history of the locomotives of the Dierks railroads can be a challenge since they were assigned to various parts of the company, including the DeQueen & Eastern Railroad, the Texas, Oklahoma & Eastern Railroad, the Dierks Lumber & Coal Company, and the Choctaw Lumber Company. They often moved between the railroads at De Queen based upon where they were needed. Additionally, some went to and from other related companies like the W. M. Waterman Lumber Company, the Florien Lumber Company, the Weyerhaeuser Timber Company, and the gypsum plant at Briar. These moves can be confusing and were often not clearly recorded. Updates and corrections on these assignments would be appreciated.

Steam Locomotives

The railroads of Dierks began with steam locomotives, and they were initially assigned to specific uses, but were commonly moved around as the logging operations and lumber production changed. Some of the steam locomotives seemed to have been lettered for almost every operation in the area. Some became famous and still survive today while others were almost invisible during their operating careers. As newer locomotives arrived and fewer logging lines were operated, some of the older locomotives were apparently sold overseas, making their final days of operations really invisible.

Published locomotive rosters generally show that the company used as many as 19 steam locomotives in the Oklahoma and Arkansas area around De Queen. This included one Shay-type geared locomotive, ten Prairie-types

(2-6-2), four 10-Wheelers (4-6-0), and four Mikado-types (2-8-2). Note that most of these steam locomotive were new, usually paid for in cash. Secondhand steam locomotives would seldom do for this prosperous operation. While some locomotives had relatively short life spans, others lasted for decades like 4-6-0 #360, which lasted in service until 1961, while 2-8-2 #226 was moved to Mountain Pine, Arkansas, and served until 1964.

However, area newspapers indicate that there were several more steam locomotives, generally obtained secondhand from area railroads. The *De Queen Bee* newspaper reported heavily on the locomotive acquisitions, but seldom provided technical data about the locomotives, or their histories. The first report appeared in the March 16, 1900, issue which stated "Don't be alarmed if you hear an unfamiliar tone among the din of whistles in the factory district. The DeQueen & Eastern's new locomotive has a fine large voice, and when it speaks will use it for De Queen." The April 13th issue reported that DeQueen & Eastern No. 9 had been steamed up and was being tested. Locomotive #9 was soon used to pull the first train of logs over the De-Queen & Eastern Railroad.

The issue published on September 6, 1901, reported that the "DeQueen & Eastern has purchased a new locomotive to meet the traffic demands on the line. No. 9 is an all right hustler but the big mill eats up the timber faster than one engine can haul it in." In October, it was reported that the "new locomotive for the DeQueen & Eastern has arrived and will be put into service at once." On January 17, 1902, it was reported that the "DeQueen & Eastern installed its third locomotive this week."

Another steam locomotive was discussed during June and July of 1902. DeQueen & Eastern engineer J. W. McKee was sent to Atlanta to inspect a "six-driver Mogul of modern pattern." During early July, McKee arrived with the new locomotive for the DeQueen & Eastern, considered to be "a valuable addition to the rolling stock of the road" and needed to "facilitate the handling of traffic." At the time, the Southern Iron & Equipment Company of Atlanta was advertising "locomotives, narrow and standard gauge, Mogul and other types, overhauled and ready for service." However, the DeQueen & Eastern isn't listed as being a customer in the remaining records of the company.

During the second half of 1903, the *De Queen Bee* reported on the arrival of several more steam locomotives. In early August, Shay No. 100 arrived, which the newspaper later described as having "driving wheels driven by a beveled gear mechanism instead of ordinary driving rods." On October 2, 1903, the newspaper included a statement that a "new locomotive for the DeQueen & Eastern is expected to arrive soon. The road is now operating five locomotives." This was followed up on December 25th with the statement that the railroad "last Tuesday received a handsome new locomotive." This was likely Alco-built No. 350.

In the July 22, 1904, issue, the newspaper reported that "locomotive No. 21 is on the blocks in the shops under-going a thorough reconstruction." Little is known of this locomotive except that it was destroyed in the shops when they burned in June 1907.

The newspaper continued to report on the delivery of new steam locomotives, including a short article in the December 1, 1905, issue. "A handsome new locomotive for the DeQueen & Eastern R.R. arrived in this city from Philadelphia Saturday night [November 25, 1905]. No. 200 is on the name plate, and it was finished in October of this year by the Baldwin Locomotive Works. Few roads in the country of the size of the DeQueen & Eastern are as well equipped as it is with rolling stock, and the increasing traffic seems to require constant addition."

The January 25, 1907, *De Queen Bee* included information on another new locomotive, "which will be put into service about February 15. This makes seven locomotives for the D.Q. & E., an excellent equipment for the amount of mileage." This included four new steam locomotives (Nos. 100, 200, 201, and 350) and three secondhand ones. The next year, No. 9 was "disposed of and was taken to Florine," actually Florien, Louisiana. Shay No. 100 followed about a year later. A strange report was published in the February 25, 1910, issue that stated "M. G. Bock returned this morning from a visit to Tennessee, where it is reported he purchased six new eighty-five ton compound locomotives for use on the DeQueen & Eastern railroad." No such locomotives were purchased.

Despite all of these newspaper reports, little clear documentation about these early secondhand locomotives is known. Locomotive No. 9 was the early star of Dierks Lumber and its DeQueen & Eastern Railroad. Because of this, it was often reported upon in the local newspaper. No. 9 was the first locomotive of the DeQueen & Eastern Railroad. Based upon a photo, it was built by the Rogers Locomotive Company as a 4-4-0. Some sources report that it was built by 1890 and acquired from the Kansas City, Pittsburg & Gulf Railroad in 1900, about the same time that the KCP&G became the Kansas City Southern. Locomotive #9 arrived at De Queen about March 1900 and hauled the first load of logs to the De Queen sawmill pond on May 25, 1900. In 1908, #9 was sent to the Sabine & Eastern Railway at Florien, Louisiana.

The more modern steam locomotives, generally bought new by the company, have better documentation. The steam locomotive numbering was not based upon its assigned ownership, instead it was based upon the wheel arrangement and the order of acquisition. Therefore, the numbers of the locomotives of Dierks Lumber, Choctaw

Lumber, DQ&E, and TO&E were mixed together. This can cause a great deal of confusion and probably no roster includes all of the changes that actually took place over the years.

The ownership confusion seemed to have even impacted the Chief Inspector of Locomotive Boilers of the Interstate Commerce Commission. For the fiscal year ending June 30, 1921, it was stated that there were 15 locomotives reported by the Texas, Oklahoma & Eastern, and that six were inspected and four were defective. No locomotives were shown to be owned by the DeQueen & Eastern.

This photo from the December 25, 1920, issue of the *American Lumberman* shows some of the modern steam locomotives used by Dierks and its railroads. Locomotive #360 had just been acquired and lasted until the end of steam. When it was retired, #360 was donated to Queen Wilhelmina State Park in Arkansas and placed on display in 1963.

The information below for each locomotive includes its assigned number, the type or wheel arrangement, the builder and its construction number (CN), and the build date assigned. It also includes other information related to the ownership history and any special design features.

No.	Type	Builder	CN	Build Date

#100 2-truck Shay Lima 802 July 29, 1903

This locomotive was a 45-ton, 2-truck Shay, built as a Class B45-2 for the Dierks Lumber & Coal Company. Photos show it to later be DeQueen & Eastern #100. In 1907, it was leased to the Cleveland-McLeod Lumber Company (Little River Valley Railroad) at Neal Springs, Arkansas. It later operated at the Boleyn Lumber Company, the Florien Lumber Company (owned by the Dierks family), and the Brown Lumber Company, all in Louisiana. It then went to George E. Dilley & Son in Palestine, Texas, where it was scrapped during the 1940s.

#200 2-6-2 Burnham, Williams & Co. (Baldwin) 26701 October 1905

The *De Queen Bee* of December 1, 1905, had a front page article about the arrival of #200, with the statement that "DeQueen & Eastern Adds to Its Rolling Stock." Baldwin records show that this locomotive was built for the DeQueen & Eastern Railroad. At the time it was described as having small drivers for operating on 30 miles of mainline track. In 1910, it was moved to the Waterman Lumber & Supply Company. This timber company operated in northeast Texas and started as the W. M. Waterman Lumber Company in 1905. By 1908, Hans Dierks was president of the firm, which operated three sawmills and a tap line and logging railroad. The operation closed during the late 1910s. Company records indicate that the locomotive was sold to the Murfreesboro-Nashville Railway (Nashville, Arkansas), which became the Murfreesboro & Nashville Railroad in 1947.

This damaged photo from the Keith McKinney Collection at the Sevier County Museum shows D&E #200, which also operated for the Waterman Lumber & Supply Company.

#201   2-6-2   Burnham, Williams & Co. (Baldwin) 30010 January 1907

Baldwin records show that this locomotive was built for the DeQueen & Eastern, and was essentially identical to locomotive #200. In 1910, it was transferred to the wholly owned subsidiary Texas, Oklahoma & Eastern Railroad. Retired and sold for export.

#202   2-6-2   Burnham, Williams & Co. (Baldwin) 35596 November 1911

Baldwin records show that this locomotive was built for the DeQueen & Eastern and was essentially identical to locomotives #200 and #201. It was almost directly assigned to the Texas, Oklahoma & Eastern Railroad. Sold for export to South America.

#203   2-6-2   Baldwin   37523 February 1912

This locomotive was built for the Texas, Oklahoma & Eastern, and was identical to one also built at the time for the Waterman Lumber & Supply Company. Baldwin used the same design as used earlier for DeQueen & Eastern #202. Sold for export to South America.

#204 2-6-2 Baldwin   37522 February 1912

Identical to TO&E #203, this locomotive was built for the Waterman Lumber & Supply Company, also owned by the Dierks family. It later joined other Prairie-type locomotives on the DeQueen & Eastern Railroad. Some photos also show it lettered for the Choctaw Lumber Company. Sold for export to South America.

Here, Choctaw Lumber Company #204 heads up a log train somewhere on the Clebit Logging Line. This photo was featured in the December 25, 1920, issue of the *American Lumberman.*

#205 2-6-2 Alco-Schenectady   54584 April 1914

The February 1914 issue of *Railway and Locomotive Engineering* reported that the "Texas, Oklahoma & Eastern has ordered 2 freight locomotives from the American Locomotive Company." However, the two locomotives built by Alco that year (#205 and #351) left the factory lettered for the DeQueen & Eastern Railroad. By the 1930s, #205 had been transferred to the Oklahoma & Rich Mountain Railroad, another Dierks operation. This railroad operated between the Kansas City Southern at Page, Oklahoma, and Pine Valley, Oklahoma, from 1926 until 1942. When the Oklahoma & Rich Mountain closed, #205 was sold to the Murfreesboro-Nashville Railway, which became the Murfreesboro & Nashville Railroad in 1947. M&N #205 was scrapped in 1952.

#206   2-6-2   Alco-Schenectady   57437 March 1917
The April 27, 1917, issue of the *De Queen Bee* reported that the "DeQueen & Eastern railroad has received a 50-ton freight engine, which will be put into operation at once. The engine was purchased from the American Locomotive Company of Schenectady, N.Y." This locomotive (some sources give the construction number as 57434, but that is a Pittsburgh & Lake Erie 4-6-2) was built for the Texas, Oklahoma & Eastern, and later assigned to the Dierks Lumber & Coal Company. It was sold and became Ferrocarril Mexicano del Pacifico #5, then in 1969 it became Compañía Industrial Azucarera SA (a sugar mill company known as CIASA) #105, both in Mexico.

#207   2-6-2   Baldwin   45549 May 1917
TO&E #207 was essentially identical to #203, although built five years later. Like all of the Prairie locomotives, it featured small drivers and could only be considered to be a mid-sized logging locomotive. It was later assigned to the DeQueen & Eastern Railroad. This locomotive was preserved and is displayed at the southeast corner of the State Fairgrounds in Tulsa, Oklahoma, lettered for Dierks Forests, Inc.

Former Dierks #207 (2-6-2) was assigned at one time or another to both the Texas, Oklahoma & Eastern and the DeQueen & Eastern railroads. Today, it is on display at the State Fairgrounds in Tulsa, Oklahoma. This photo dates from 1990, not long after a fresh coat of black paint was applied to the locomotive.

#208   2-6-2   Baldwin   47437 December 1917

DeQueen & Eastern #208 was a larger, coal-burning locomotive built to move freight across the mainline of the railroad. By this time, cars were heavier and loads moved greater distances, so this more modern design was necessary to keep the railroad moving. This locomotive was later used at Mountain Pine, Arkansas. Retired and scrapped.

#209 2-6-2 Baldwin   53269 May 1920

This was the last Prairie-type steam locomotive built for Dierks. Built as Texas, Oklahoma & Eastern #209, it was essentially identical to DQ&E #208 and featured a coal-burning firebox, unlike many of the earlier steam locomotives which were oil-burners. Retired and scrapped.

This photo of TO&E #209 shows it being put back on the track after derailing with a log train on Spur #1, the Clebit Logging Line. Courtesy of the Keith McKinney Collection at the Sevier County Museum.

#225   2-8-2   Baldwin   38807 November 1912

While considered a smaller Mikado-type steam locomotive, Texas, Oklahoma & Eastern #225 was large for the railroad. It was primarily used on mainline trains until later in its career when it handled log trains on the two main logging spurs. Retired and scrapped.

#226   2-8-2   Baldwin   60005 May 1927

This was one of two Mikado-type locomotives built for the Dierks Lumber & Coal Company in 1927. Both were designed to move larger trains over the steepest grades on the logging railroads, in some cases as steep as 6%. This locomotive was originally assigned to De Queen, and later operated on the Clebit Logging Line out of Wright City. These were relatively small standard-gauge 2-8-2s that lasted until the end of steam in the 1960s, lettered for Dierks Forests, Inc. Locomotive #226 was donated for display in the city park of Benton, Arkansas, and was moved from Hot Springs to Benton by the Rock Island Railroad in 1965. It then was moved to the Eureka Springs & North Arkansas tourist railroad in 1988, where it remains on display.

Dierks #226 (2-8-2) was acquired by the Eureka Springs & North Arkansas tourist railroad in 1988. While there were plans to operate the steam locomotive, it has remained on display. Here it is shown next to the railroad's wooden business car, one of a number of pieces of rail equipment that have been located on that railroad.

#227 2-8-2 Baldwin   60006 May 1927

This steam locomotive is identical to Dierks #226 and was used for many years on the logging lines at Dierks, and then Mountain Pine, Arkansas. Originally lettered for the Dierks Lumber & Coal Company, it was later lettered for Dierks Forests, Inc. It ended its career operating over the Clebit Logging Line at Wright City, Oklahoma, with its last overhaul taking place in 1962 and its last run in 1963. In 1972, Weyerhaeuser donated it to Broken Bow, where it is still on display next to the depot.

Dierks #227 is one of four Dierks steam locomotives that still exist, and is on display at Broken Bow, Oklahoma, along with a wooden log car.

Information about the construction of Dierks #227 can still be found on the steam locomotive. This Baldwin builders plate shows the construction number (60006) and build date (May 1927). The Superheater Company plate can also be found elsewhere on the locomotive.

#350 4-6-0 Alco-Pittsburgh 29438 December 1903

This ten-wheeler was built by the American Locomotive Company for the DeQueen & Eastern Railroad. Along with Shay #100, this was the first new steam locomotive built for the Dierks logging operations. While generally shown to be working mainline freight trains, it also hauled log trains when needed. In May 1910, it hauled a log loader and more than 20 log cars from De Queen to Bismark to add logging capacity for the Choctaw Lumber Company. It was retired and scrapped.

#351 4-6-0 Alco-Schenectady 54585 April 1914

This locomotive was initially painted for the Texas, Oklahoma & Eastern. While generally shown to be working mainline freight trains, it also hauled log trains when needed. It was reportedly retired and scrapped in 1958.

#355 4-6-0 Baldwin 40320 August 1913

This locomotive was originally built as Little Rock, Maumelle & Western #101. It was sold in a foreclosure sale to the Dierks Lumber & Coal Company on September 29, 1922. It later was assigned to the Choctaw Lumber Company. Retired and scrapped.

#360 4-6-0 American Locomotive Company 62204 July 1920

This ten-wheeler was built by Alco for the Texas, Oklahoma & Eastern as a mainline locomotive, often pulling the regular mixed train across the railroad. On June 30, 1954, it was transferred to Dierks, and then moved to Queen Wilhelmina State Park in 1963, where it is still on display.

Steam locomotive #360 operated for Dierks for about 40 years, but has been at Queen Wilhelmina State Park in Arkansas for more than 60 years. It sits on top of the mountain near the campgrounds, with a walkway allowing tours of the cab.

Displayed at Queen Wilhelmina State Park in Arkansas, the south-facing steam locomotive provides plenty of opportunities for photography of its classic front.

#375 2-8-2 Baldwin   38094 August 1912

This steam locomotive was bought by the DeQueen & Eastern because of the construction of the Texas, Oklahoma & Eastern. Like TO&E #225, it was acquired to handle many of the mainline trains. Retired and scrapped.

Although not a steam locomotive, the railroad had other steam-powered equipment for many years. This is Wrecker Crane #22, built by Industrial Works in 1920. Industrial Works of Bay City, Michigan, produced the first commercial steam railroad wrecking crane in 1883, and became the Industrial Brownhoist Corporation in 1927. The company went through several owners before closing for good in 1983. This crane was built in 1920 as Kansas City Southern #3, assigned to Heavener, Oklahoma. It was acquired by the DeQueen & Eastern, and the boiler was rebuilt in 1977. The existence of asbestos caused another rebuild, but the crane was never used again. The crane was scrapped in 2017 after sitting around the De Queen yard for several decades.

Diesel Locomotives

The DeQueen & Eastern was an early user of internal combustion engines (using both gasoline and diesel fuels), building a series of motor buses and similar vehicles to replace steam-pulled passenger trains and to move supplies and employees to and from the woods. However, it wasn't until after World War II that the railroad acquired its first large internal combustion locomotives – two former U.S. Army Whitcomb 65-tonners. Two more switch engines were acquired during the 1950s, and then a series of modern mid-horsepower locomotives were bought during the 1960s and 1970s. To most people who have only known the railroad over the past 50 years, strings of locomotives built by EMD (GP35s, GP38s, GP40s, and GP40-2s) are the image of the company.

By the early 1960s, the steam shop at De Queen had been replaced by a diesel shop, with all of the machinery necessary to maintain a locomotive fleet. These shops range from very modern buildings to an original brick structure from the earliest times of the railroad. The quality of the work performed here allows the company to contract out their services to other area rail operations.

Like with the steam locomotives, the locomotive numbering was not based upon the assigned ownership of the unit, instead it was based upon the order of acquisition. Therefore, locomotives of Dierks, DQ&E, and TO&E are mixed together. To differentiate the diesel locomotives from the steam locomotives, the numbers started with "D" for diesel. Later, Weyerhaeuser kept the letter, but used it to designate the locomotives assigned to De Queen, Arkansas.

The following information describes each locomotive by its model, builder, builder construction number, and build date. It then traces the ownership of the locomotive. With the ownership of the railroad by Patriot Rail, which currently owns more than 30 railroads, locomotives now move freely between the various lines. The railroad also uses leased locomotives from several firms. Because of this, the diesel locomotive roster is for those locomotives specifically owned by the DeQueen & Eastern and Texas, Oklahoma & Eastern railroads and assigned the "D" numbering system. For those wanting to see color pictures of the DeQueen & Eastern diesel roster, check out Mike Condren's Railroad Pages online.

D-1   65-Ton, Whitcomb #60451, built 6/1944 as U.S. Army #8445, to Dierks #D-1 12/1947, assigned to Dierks Treating Plant 1959, scrapped 1983.

D-2   65-Ton, Whitcomb #60468, built 7/1944 as U.S. Army #8462, to Dierks #D-2 12/1947, assigned to the Mountain Pine operation, scrapped 1983.

D-3   SW8, EMD #13952, built 3/1951 as DQ&E #D-3, to TO&E #D-3 11/1977, to Silcott Equipment in 1985.

D-4   SW900, EMD #19528, built 5/1954 as DQ&E #D-4, to Dierks Forest #D-4, to TO&E #D-4 11/1977, then to Weyerhaeuser Timber Company #D-4. To Mid-Am Equipment (Mesa, Arizona) 10/94. It then went through the hands of the David J. Joseph Company, Relco, and became GATX Rail Locomotive Group (GMTX) #704.

D-5   SW1200, EMD #25731, built 2/1960 as DQ&E #D-5, to Nucor Steel (Blytheville, Arkansas) 8/94, to Incoal Company/ArcelorMittal (INLX 114) at East Chicago, Indiana.

D-6   GP35, EMD #29359, built 5/1964 as DQ&E #D-6, to Kiamichi Railroad 10/1996, to Arkansas Midland #2500.

D-7   GP40, EMD #31855, built 8/1966 as DQ&E #D-7.

D-8   65-Ton, Porter #7655, built 8/1944 as U.S. Navy #65-00177, to Dierks #D-8 in 1966, to Weyerhaeuser #D-8 at Briar gypsum plant, to James Hardie Gypsum #D-8 in 1989, sold 2009.

DeQueen & Eastern D-6 is shown working the Valliant yards in 1990. This GP35 has gone on to work various lines in Arkansas as Arkansas Midland #2500.

D&E locomotive D-7 was one of several locomotives working the De Queen North Yard in 1989. It was still on the property in 2024.

D-9 44-Ton, GE #29971, built 7/1948 as Pennsylvania #9338, to Striegel, to Dierks #D-9 in 1966, to W.A. Smith Contracting (Tatum, Texas) 9/1974.

D-10   NW2, EMD #575, built 9/1948 as Detroit, Toledo & Ironton #910, to Chicago, West Pullman & Southern #49, to Silcott, to Dierks Forests #D-10 in 1969, to TO&E #D-10 in 1969, sold in 1984.

D-11   45-Ton, GE #27700, built 10/1944 as U.S. Army #1847, to U.S. Army #8562, to Birmingham Rail & Locomotive, to Dierks #D-11 in 1971, assigned to the Valliant paper mill, to Trinity River Authority (Grande Prairie, Texas) in 1984.

D-12   GP40, EMD #36879, built 3/1971 as DQ&E #D-12, to TO&E #D-12.

Locomotive D-12 is shown switching at De Queen in 2023. While more than fifty years old, this locomotive continues to lead trains over the DeQueen & Eastern Railroad.

D-13   GP40, EMD #38244, built 9/1971 as TO&E #D-13.

D-14   GP40, EMD #38570, built 9/1971 as TO&E #D-14.

D-15   GP40-2, EMD #72654, built 12/1972 as TO&E #D-15, to Clarendon & Pittsford Railroad #306 11/2000, to GMTX 3204.

On a sunny March day in 1990, TO&E D-15 leads a three-unit consist working the yards at Valliant, Oklahoma. At that time, a number of trains operated over the west end of the railroad, often pulled by multiple locomotives like this.

D-16 GP40-2, EMD #73619, built 11/1973 at TO&E #D-16. Locomotive D16 was scrapped in 2009 after it was involved in a road crossing collision at New Highway 98 coming out of the Wright City yard in 2008.

TO&E D-16 pushes interchange traffic to the Kansas City Southern in September 2000, passing KCS 1. KCS brought their executive train to De Queen as part of the DQ&E's centennial celebration.

D-17   SW9, EMD #16334, built 9/1952 as Pittsburgh & Lake Erie #8956, to P&LE #1239, to TO&E #D-17 3/1974, to DQ&E #D-17, to Western Railroad 1/1985.

D-18   SW9, EMD #16339, built 9/1952 as Pittsburgh & Lake Erie #8961, to P&LE #1234, to TO&E #D-18 3/1974, assigned to the Craig facility, to Weyerhaeuser D-18, to VMV in 1984.

D-19   SW9, EMD #16338, built 9/1953 as Pittsburgh & Lake Erie #8960, to P&LE #1235, to TO&E #D-19 3/1974, assigned to the Valliant facility, to Weyerhaeuser D-19, to VMV in 1984.

D-20   GP40-2, EMD #74604-1, built 9/1974 as TO&E #D-20, to DQ&E #D-20.

Locomotive D-20, still carrying its TO&E lettering, was still in service on the railroad in 2023, shown here working at Dierks.

D-21   SW9, EMD #18851, built 11/1953 as Union Pacific #1863, to Chrome Crankshaft for rebuilding at ICG's Paducah shop, to TO&E #D-21 7/1977, to Weyerhaeuser

D-21 at Mountain Pine (AR), to Kaiser Permanente Cement #881-005.

Locomotive D-21 is shown in 1991 working Weyerhaeuser's Mountain Pine sawmill, located near Hot Springs, Arkansas.

D-22 GP35, EMD #30136, built 4/1965 as Southern Pacific #7729, to SP #6626, wrecked 7/1973 and rebuilt by Morrison-Knudsen to Weyerhaeuser #308 10/1974, to TO&E #D-22 3/1980, to Kiamichi #3502 10/1996, to Arkansas Midland #2502.

TO&E D-22, still in a coat of blue paint, was parked at the Dierks depot on February 16, 1991. This locomotive later was used by the Kiamichi and the Arkansas Midland railroads.

D-23 GP40, EMD #34339, built 10/1968 as Penn Central #3162, to Conrail #3162, to TO&E #D-23 10/1983, rebuilt by VMV in 1984.

D-24 GP40, EMD #34300, built 8/1968 as Penn Central #3123, to Conrail #3123, to TO&E #D-24 10/1983. Now painted in Patriot Rail blue.

D-25 GP40, EMD #33505, built 10/1967 as New York Central #3094, to Penn Central #3094, to Conrail #3094, to TO&E #D-25 8/1984, rebuilt by VMV in 1990.

On March 6, 2024, locomotives D-23, D-24 and D-25 were coupled together and working the local at Dierks.

D-26 Self-Propelled Crane, Weyerhaeuser, to DQ&E #D-26.

D-27 GP38-2, EMD #796388-1, built 1/1981 as Curtis, Milburn & Eastern #817, to Chehalis Western #817, to DQ&E #D-27 4/1994, to TO&E #D-27.

D-28   GP38-2, EMD #796388-2, built 1/1981 as Curtis, Milburn & Eastern #818, to Chehalis Western #818, to DQ&E #D-28 4/1994, to TO&E #D-28, to Kingman Terminal in 2022.

Diesel locomotives D-29 through D-32 were all acquired by Patriot Rail and wear the company's modern blue paint. All of these locomotives have been rebuilt to GP40-2 standards and include new frames, eliminating their original frame numbers. There have also been many other locomotives leased and assigned to the DeQueen & Eastern. Many of them come from LTEX (Larry's Truck & Electric) such as #4015, which has spent some time working out of De Queen.

Another issue related to the locomotive roster is that LTEX D-32 is painted in Patriot blue and is sometimes shown as being assigned to the DeQueen & Eastern. However, it is actually located on the Georgia Northeastern Railroad, another Patriot Rail operation. It was former Southern GP38-2 5043, assigned to the Central of Georgia subsidiary. It became Norfolk Southern 5043 and then was sold to LTEX.

D-29   GP40, EMD #33262, built 8/1967 as Norfolk & Western #1371, to Norfolk Southern #1371, rebuilt to GP40-2 NS #3089, to MRIX 5/2020, to DQ&E #3089 7/2021, renumbered #D-29 1/2022.

DeQueen & Eastern D-29 is shown passing under Arkansas Highway 41 on a beautiful March day in 2023.

D-30   GP40-2, EMD #776025-15, built 12/1977 as Boston & Maine #314, to Helm Financial Corporation #509 2/1994, to Vermont Rail #303 9/1998, to GATX Corporation #3204, to S&S Sales & Leasing 9/2021, to DQ&E #D-30 1/2022.

D-31   GP40, EMD #34083, built 8/1968 as Missouri-Kansas-Texas #200, later painted as Bicentennial #200, to Union Pacific #506 8/1988, to National Railway Equipment, to Georgia Southwestern #4005, to Alabama & Gulf Coast #4005, to Bro-Tex International Metals 10/2011, to Sterling Bomba 4/2012, to Motive Power Resource #4005 and rebuilt to GP40-2, to Metro East Industries 7/2014, to Foster Townsend Rail Logistics #4005 8/2015, to DQ&E #4005, renumbered D-31 1/2023.

Mile-by-Mile Route Guide

This route guide is designed to tell the mile-by-mile history of the DeQueen & Eastern/Texas, Oklahoma & Eastern rail network. It includes information about the various communities served by the two railroads, as well as other major features such as rivers, mountains and highways. Each location is identified by a milepost as used by the railroad, which start at the west end of the line at Valliant and get larger as you travel east. It should be noted that many of these locations have had multiple mileposts. This is often because of the extension of tracks, the construction of new shippers and facilities, and improvements made on the route. Every attempt has been made to use the current name and milepost for each location.

Milepost signs like this one can be found along the railroad, and are used to describe the specific locations along the railroad. Milepost 68 is near Provo, Arkansas, close to the east end of the DeQueen & Eastern.

The route guide follows the railroad from west to east, as if you were riding a train from Valliant to De Queen and on to Perkins. Items to the left are to the north, and items to the right are to the south. This will generally be used even when the railroad turns greatly from running east-west. However, in some cases, actual directions will be used to make it clearer where a feature is located.

0.0 VALLIANT – Valliant is the west end of the De-Queen & Eastern/Texas, Oklahoma & Eastern network. While the population is only about 800, it is the home of a number of stores, restaurants, gas stations, and the Valliant School District. It is also the home of the Valliant Mill of International Paper. This mill was built by Weyerhaeuser during the early 1970s and was the largest paper mill in the world at the time. In 2008, International Paper acquired the containerboard packaging and recycling business of Weyerhaeuser for $6 billion in cash, including this mill which now employs 600 workers and produces linerboard and corrugated medium. This activity requires the DeQueen & Eastern to keep a locomotive and crew working at Valliant seven days a week.

This area was one of the first in Oklahoma to be settled due to Clear Creek, located to the west of Valliant. Initially, this was in Miller County of the Arkansas Territory. A gristmill was built on Clear Creek by 1819, and the remains can still be found southwest of town. Clear Creek was an important source of drinking water, and even served that purpose for Valliant for many years. After the land was assigned to the Choctaw Nation in 1820 as part of Indian Territory, the timber for homes and open land for farming was quickly put to use as a few of the tribe began to arrive. After the signing of the

Dancing Rabbit Creek Treaty, more than six thousand Choctaw moved from Mississippi to the region during the fall and winter of 1831-1832. Another five thousand arrived over the next year.

A unique part of the move was that residents from the three traditional districts of the Choctaw Nation generally stayed together when they settled in Indian Territory. Because of this, they kept their traditional government districts – Moshulatubbee (northeast), Pushmataha (southwest), and Apukshunnubbee (southeast). The area where Valliant was later created was part of the Apukshunnubbee District, named in honor of Chief Apukshunnubbee, a Choctaw warrior and statesman who had been district chief of the Okla Falaya District of the original Choctaw Nation. The government was based at Alikchi, located north of Wright City. While the counties have changed, this is still part of the Choctaw Nation.

In 1886, the Alice Lee Elliott Memorial Academy, a boarding school for children of freed black slaves, opened near what became Valliant. It is often forgotten that some members of the Choctaw Nation were slave owners, growing large amounts of cotton in Mississippi, and then in southeast Oklahoma. Education was still difficult to obtain in the 1880s, so the Presbyterian Board of Missions sponsored this school until 1936.

During the late 1800s, a small community grew up near here. In 1894, the community was big enough to be awarded a post office, named Fowlerville after the first postmaster, Nathaniel M. Fowler. Things changed when the Arkansas & Choctaw Railroad Company (Frisco) built through the area and the post office and town were renamed for Frank W. Valliant, chief engineer of the railroad, on June 23,

1902. The town was reorganized with a new survey and plat, performed by the railroad. The railroad immediately attracted new businesses, including a cotton gin that opened in 1903. In 1904, the town incorporated and elected its first mayor. While agriculture (cotton, grain, vegetables and cattle) was the most important local economic activity, within a decade Valliant featured a newspaper, two banks, three hotels, several cafes, and nearly 20 other businesses.

This Valliant sign hangs on the west end of the old Frisco station during March 2023.

When Valliant was founded, this area was still in Towson County, a part of the Apukshunnubbee District of the Choctaw Nation in Indian Territory. When Oklahoma became the 46th state on November 16, 1907, McCurtain County was established. Although not selected as the new county seat, Valliant grew to 656 residents by the 1910 census. Much of this growth was thanks to the purchase of large tracts of local timber by the Dierks Lumber & Coal Company. To reach this timber, Dierks started building a railroad line, grading some four miles north and east from Valiant. The company also surveyed another ten miles as part of a planned extension of the railroad from Valiant to De Queen, Arkansas.

The population grew quickly to 809 residents in 1920, but dropped back to only 608 residents by 1930 due to lower farm prices, much of the local timber being cut, and the start of the Great Depression. By 1940, the population of Valliant was 551. This trend of increased population during good times and lower populations during bad has continued to today. The population grew to 661 during World War II and the need for wooden boxes, and then dropped again during the 1950s. It jumped to 840 residents in 1970 due to the construction of the Weyerhaeuser mill, and then more as the plant expanded operations, reaching the all-time peak of 927 in the 1980 census. Since then, Valliant has seen a slow population decline, but with a jump back to 819 in the 2020 census. Today, Valliant's economy is based upon the local paper mill, travelers on U.S. Highway 70, and some local tourism due to Pine Creek Lake and the Pine Creek Wildlife Management Area.

The Arkansas & Choctaw Railway Company

Valliant owes much of its existence to the Arkansas & Choctaw Railway Company. The Arkansas & Choctaw Railway, which eventually connected Hope, Arkansas, and Ardmore, Oklahoma, was incorporated in Arkansas on August 31, 1895. The railroad company proposed to build and operate a railroad from Ashdown, Arkansas, on what later became the Kansas City Southern (KCS) mainline, westward for seventy miles through the Choctaw Nation of Indian Territory. Permission was received from Congress to build across the Indian Territory lands in 1896.

Construction took place in several locations, and initially the Arkansas & Choctaw also had trackage rights to operate between Texarkana and Ashdown over the KCS. The Kiamichi River bridge was apparently a challenge as several announcements were made about opening the line first in March 1902, then April and May. Meanwhile, the line was being extended eastward from Ashdown as far as Hope, Arkansas, with surveys being made all the way to the Mississippi River. Newspaper reports from late May 1902 stated that the bridge over the Kiamichi River had been completed and train service between Ashdown and Hugo would begin operating by June 1, 1902. In reality, the first Arkansas & Choctaw train crossed the new bridge over the Kiamichi River on June 4, 1902.

The next several months saw a number of changes to the Arkansas & Choctaw Railway at the corporate level. In late July, James Campbell, president of the Arkansas & Choctaw, and Benjamin Franklin Yoakum, president of the St. Louis & San Francisco, announced that the Arkansas & Choctaw (88 miles of track between Ashdown and Hugo) would be controlled and operated by the St. Louis & San Francisco (Frisco) effective August 1, 1902. Full control was obtained for $5 million when the Frisco purchased the certificates of the Arkansas & Choctaw Construction Company, which was building the railroad. The railroad's operation was assigned to the St. Louis, San Francisco & New Orleans Railroad Company, which replaced the Arkansas & Choctaw name during a foreclosure sale on October 2, 1902. The entire operation was simplified on April 30,

1907, when the St. Louis, San Francisco & New Orleans Railroad Company was sold to the St. Louis & San Francisco Railroad Company. This company became the St. Louis-San Francisco Railway Company (Frisco) on September 15, 1916.

In 1990, the Frisco's Valliant station was still used and looked like it was well taken care of.

In 2023, the former Frisco station barely stands at Valliant, Oklahoma. Despite large holes in the roof, the cinder block and asbestos siding structure still stands straight, but is surrounded by trash.

Across the Kiamichi Railroad tracks from the depot at Valliant is Railroad Street.

For those looking for a sign of the old Frisco, the shell of their depot still stands east of the Dalton Avenue grade crossing at Valliant near Frisco Milepost 710.2. This area used to be full of rail shippers, including from west to east, a cotton seed warehouse, bottling plant, hay warehouse, cotton platform, and the railroad stock pens. The cotton platform was used by the Valliant Cotton Gin Company, which was across North Railroad Street. Further west at Milepost 710.0 is the TO&E diamond.

Before the mill was constructed, there was only a wye here to the north that connected with the mainline of the Texas, Oklahoma & Eastern. The Frisco had rights to use the wye so it could interchange traffic with the Dierks railroad. By the time *St. Louis - San Francisco Railway Company System Time Table No. 1, Effective Sunday, October 17, 1971*, was published, there was a railroad crossing at grade at Milepost 710.0 known simply as T.O.E. The crossing was protected by a gate, with its normal position against the conflicting route (the TO&E). The Frisco also had a note about operations over the wye. "Trains will use both legs of wye and T.O.E. main track to T.O.E. MP 1-2, Valliant."

After operating as an independent railroad for 64 years, the St. Louis-San Francisco Railway was acquired and merged into Burlington Northern on November 21, 1980. As the railroad looked to sell off its lighter-used lines, 230 miles of track in Arkansas, Oklahoma and Texas were sold to StatesRail, which created the Kiamichi Railroad, which started operations on July 22, 1987. During January 2002, StatesRail was acquired by RailAmerica, which was acquired by Genesee & Wyoming in December 2012. The Kiamichi Railroad still operates east-west through Valliant, providing an important connection for the DeQueen & Eastern Railroad, and a link to the BNSF rail system.

During early 2023, Kiamichi Railroad #4080 was pulling a freight eastbound, approaching Fort Towson and heading to Valliant for interchange with the DeQueen & Eastern. Less than a minute earlier, the train passed under the Western Farmers Electric Cooperative line from Valliant.

The DeQueen & Eastern at Valliant

The DeQueen & Eastern's operations at Valliant started with the Choctaw Lumber Company (closely related to the Dierks Lumber & Coal Company) and its need to reach its nearby timber. Some railroad construction took place by 1909, but by Dierks Lumber & Coal. Several announcements were made that four miles of track were graded that year, and that ten more miles had been surveyed as an effort to connect Valliant with De Queen. To make the effort official, the Texas, Oklahoma & Eastern Railroad (TO&E) was incorporated in Oklahoma on October 21, 1910. Actually controlled by the DeQueen & Eastern, the railroad began operating in June 1911.

Things became busy at Valliant when the railroad was completed as rail transportation was acquired for inbound raw materials (timber and chemicals) and outbound finished materials (lumber and pulpwood). The small station at Valliant was a busy one, handling the interchange with the St. Louis & San Francisco Railroad (Frisco). For years, it was also a telephone station that handled company communications. Something unique about the Dierks railroads is that they used telephones from the start to transmit train orders, even as most railroads still used telegraph.

Passenger service on the DQ&E/TO&E was never heavy, but it did operate during the early years. Train No. 9, which operated daily except Sunday in 1925, was scheduled to arrive at Valliant from De Queen at 3:25pm. It would then depart as train No. 10 at 4:35pm. The Sunday-only No. 1 train would arrive at 3:15pm, and depart as No. 2 at 4:15pm.

By 1947, the Dierks mainline rail system had almost reached maturity. In that year, the Texas, Oklahoma & Eastern had a 16-car siding at Valliant and a full wye to connect with the Frisco line. To handle train orders and other paperwork, the railroad showed that there was a day telephone office here.

In 1969, Dierks Forests, Inc. (Dierks Lumber & Coal Company until 1954) sold its operations to the Weyerhaeuser Company. Weyerhaeuser built 20 miles of new tracks – yards and industry tracks – after the purchase. Most of these tracks were because the traffic at Valliant greatly increased with the construction of the new Weyerhaeuser container board plant in 1971. Suddenly, the TO&E had a major customer at Valliant. This led to an expansion of the railroad, which built across the Arkansas & Choctaw line to reach the mill yard. The mill features a large number of railroad tracks, all served from the large DQ&E/TO&E yard on the east side of the plant. Because of the volume of traffic, the railroad has a car shop south of the diamond that is used to repair freight cars, especially the boxcars used to move paper from the mill. As of 2024, the railroad is building eight additional tracks at the car shop in Valliant.

The DQE/TOE Railroad Shop is currently located south of the Valliant Diamond and is used to repair freight cars.

The new Valliant crossing uses a gate to protect the trains of the two railroads. Interchange tracks are in the southwest and northwest quadrants, and Valliant has been the base of some train operations since at least the 1970s. In 1979, Valliant housed a train register station and bulletin books, allowing crews to start and end their day here. The small office building was once located on the northwest corner of the diamond where the crossing gate still stands.

This gate, aligned across the Kiamichi Railroad tracks in this photo, protects the various train movements through the Valliant Crossing.

Heading north from the diamond with the Kiamichi Railroad, which is essentially Milepost 0.0 on the TO&E, the railroad passes around the west side of Valliant at an elevation of slightly more than 500 feet. There was once a large wye on the north side of the Kiamichi, with the west leg still in place for interchange business. The railroad crosses U.S. Highway 70 (Wilson Street) at grade at Milepost 0.1. Because Dierks built their railroad several decades after the Arkansas & Choctaw, most of the rail shippers were located on what became the Kiamichi Railroad. The majority of the downtown businesses were located along Dalton Avenue north of Wilson Street, five blocks to the east of the Texas, Oklahoma & Eastern Railroad.

Heading north and then east towards Wright City, the railroad first climbs to an elevation of 545 feet and then drops down to the Little River, which is about 400 feet above sea level.

In 1990, crane D-21 was found parked at Valliant, Oklahoma.

International Paper's Valliant Mill

The Valliant Mill employs approximately 600 workers and produces linerboard and corrugated medium for produce containers (fruits and vegetables), meat/poultry packaging, and computer and appliance boxes. When the mill opened in 1972, it was the largest paper mill in the world. The mill features a full chipping mill so it can support local timber production. The facility has its own power plant which produces electricity from black liquor (wood waste biomass) and natural gas. Excess electricity is sold to the local power grid.

This view of the International Paper Valliant Mill is from the north and shows the electrical plant.

This sign for the International Paper mill stands next to the Kiamichi Railroad a short distance west of the diamond with the DeQueen & Eastern.

The mill faces to the west and the railroad has a complex system of tracks and yards on the east side of the property. Heading south from the diamond, the railroad has a switch to the interchange track, passes several offices and warehouses, and then a small car shop, all located west of the TO&E. A track also curves into this area just before the TO&E tracks curve to the east and enters a large seven-track yard. The east end of the yard is located immediately west of Section Line Road, also known as Valliant Bypass Road. There are two tracks to the east that are used as interchange tracks, with a switch on the Kiamichi mainline further to the east at Robins Egg Lane.

From the west side of the yard, a long rail lead heads to the northwest, off which a series of spur tracks serve different parts of the plant. These include chemicals, warehousing and outbound shipments, and various inbound dry shipments. A dozen tracks form a small yard on the south side of the plant. Two large rotary car dumps to unload carloads of woodchips are found at the west end of this yard. Historically, several locomotives and crews could be kept busy working the car dumps and yard.

It must be noted that there is essentially no access to any of this railroad facility as it is all on railroad or International Paper property. All roads are gated or clearly signed for no trespassing. Only Section Line Road provides any viewing.

Because the yards east of the International Paper mill are used by both the DeQueen & Eastern and Kiamichi railroads, this sign alerts train crews to the ways to contact the other railroad.

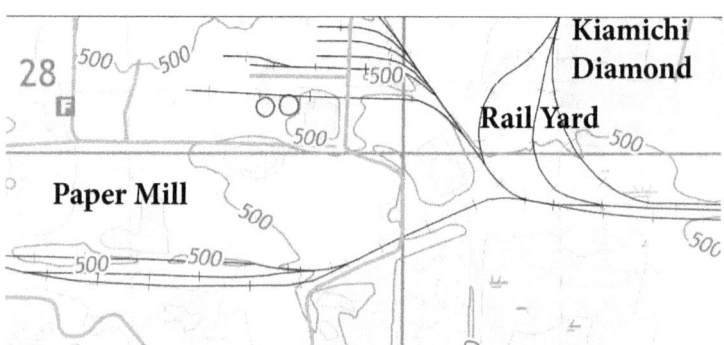

Today, Valliant is a complex network of tracks serving the IP paper mill. *Millerton (OK) Quadrangle – 2022, U.S. Department of the Interior, U.S. Geological Survey.* https://ngmdb.usgs.gov/ht-bin/tv_browse. pl?id=8b5b4a0cdf8dee199dd9e9218c139a6d

0.2 **NORTH VALLIANT** – This is the south switch of North Valliant, a yard used to switch cars, handle interchange with the Kiamichi Railroad, and make up trains for along the TO&E rail line. It was a significant facility until the new yard was built on the east side of the paper and board mill. Today, there is a single track on each side of the TO&E mainline, each long enough to hold a large number of cars (60 cars on the west track and 40 cars on the east track).

This view from U.S. Highway 70 shows the tracks of the Texas, Oklahoma & Eastern as they pass through the North Valliant Yard.

1.3 **WFEC JUNCTION** – At the north end of the North Valliant yard is a junction with a relatively new line, the WFEC Railroad Company. Western Farmers Electric Cooperative (WFEC), organized in 1941, is a generation and transmission cooperative that provides electric service to 21 member cooperatives and Altus Air Force Base.

In July of 2000, the tracks of the Western Farmer's line to Valliant still looked new, as shown from this hirail view. This small crossing with cattle guards was installed to allow a local rancher to move his herds from field to field.

This sign marks one of the entrances to the Western Farmers Electric Cooperative Hugo Plant, once served by the DeQueen & Eastern via the WFEC Railroad from Valliant.

West of here near Fort Townson is the big Western Farmers Electric Cooperative Hugo Plant which burns Wyoming coal to produce electricity. The plant was completed in 1982 and included six miles of rail line, and the company acquired 330 rail cars to move the coal. The coal initially arrived via Burlington Northern/Kiamichi in the company's coal cars (WFCX), but in 1995, the power company received approval to construct and operate "a 14-mile line of railroad" from "the Western Farmers Electric Cooperative's Hugo Generating Station loop track, cross a line of the Kiamichi Railroad Company, and then extend east to connect with a line of the Texas, Oklahoma & Eastern Railroad Company near Valliant, OK." In early 1997, an announcement was published in *Bloomberg* (February 13, 1997) about a change in operations that came about due to this construction.

Kansas City Southern Railway (KCS), Union Pacific and the Texas, Oklahoma & Eastern (TO&E) railroads today announced they have been awarded a contract to haul Wyoming's Powder River Basin coal to the Western Farmers Electric Cooperative (WFEC) generation facility near Ft. Towson, Okla.

The contract calls for Union Pacific to haul the coal from Wyoming to Kansas City, where it is interchanged with KCS. KCS will take the coal to DeQueen, Ark., where it will be interchanged with the TO&E. The TO&E will be able to serve the facility from Valliant, Okla., over a 14-mile spur WFEC expects to have completed in April.

Because of the size of the coal trains, the De-Queen & Eastern installed an automatic turnout at this location. Trains approaching the turnout could use their radio to dial a code that would line the switch in the direction needed by the train.

For several years, coal arrived 3 to 4 times per week, mainly over the D&E/TO&E via KCS and UP at Kansas City. However, changes took place by 2002 when the Kiamichi Railroad gained overhead trackage rights on the WFEC Railroad line. On January 1, 2012, the WFEC Railroad Company granted limited nonexclusive overhead trackage rights to the Kiamichi Railroad between Milepost 0.0 at Western Farmers Electric Cooperative Hugo electric generating station and milepost 14.98, where WFECR connects to the line of the Texas, Oklahoma & Eastern Railroad Company. The new agreement allowed the Kiamichi Railroad to serve any Western Farmers' facility that could locate along the line. This led to the Kiamichi Railroad being declared the primary operating railroad on the WFEC Railroad.

2.0   EAST END VALLIANT YARD LIMITS – The track to the west to the Valliant Mill is all covered by yard limits. For years, the railroad was operated by a mix of yard limits and "Block Register Territory." On August 17, 2017, the railroad replaced the Block Register Territory practice with "Track Warrant Control." It then went back to block limits, which were used until early 2023 when track warrant control began.

Railroad-east towards De Queen, the DQ&E/TO&E heads to the northeast through a mix of woods and farms. It also crosses a number of southward-flowing streams.

This March 2023 view is of the Kiamichi Railroad passing under the Western Farmers Electric Cooperative line from Valliant.

3.2   FELKER – This location is easy to find as it is near the Woodpecker Trail grade crossing. To the southeast is Felker Road while to the northwest is Bobwhite Lane. When construction on the Texas, Oklahoma & Eastern began, grading reached here quickly and Felker was one of the first recognized points on the railroad. It has sometimes been used for log loading. The area was also the site of the Four Mile Boarding Camp, used to house loggers and track workers during the early years of the railroad.

The name Felker came from the Felker family which moved from South Carolina to this general area in 1890. A. W. "Bud" Felker was a U.S. government surveyor who helped survey the lands of the Choctaw and Chickasaw Nations. When McCurtain County was founded in 1907, he was elected as the county's first official surveyor. In early 1921, Bud Felker was made sheriff, a position he held until August 13, 1922, when he was killed by a suspect in several local murders.

This Felker Road sign is one of the few reminders of the former station found at Milepost 3.2.

4.3   WHITE OAK CREEK BRIDGE – This small stream forms northwest of Valliant and flows into the Little River, about a mile east of here. The bridge consists of 145 feet of timber pile trestle spans.

4.7   OLD STATE HIGHWAY 98 – Old State Highway 98 connects Valliant with Wright City. State Highway 98 was commissioned sometime in 1953 to connect Wright City with U.S. Highway 70. Like most highways, its route has been extended and changed over the years. In 1960, the route was changed to connect Wright City with Valliant, but moved to the east in 1975, connecting with U.S. Highway 70 near Millerton.

Here, the railroad turns to the east to head towards De Queen, Arkansas.

5.2 **LITTLE RIVER BRIDGE** – The Little River Bridge was finished in October 1909 as part of the railroad's initial construction from Valliant to Bismark (Wright City). The railroad crosses the Little River using a six-span deck plate girder structure. An earlier bridge was a through truss bridge that was 308 feet long in 1926, according to the Interstate Commerce Commission. The larger bridges on this line consisted of through truss bridges, a common design when the railroad was built. However, as trains have gotten heavier and the bridges aged, many have been replaced by deck plate girder spans. For example, in 2015, Patriot Rail announced a budget of $600,000 to conduct bridge work across its system, predominantly on the DeQueen & Eastern. During the fall of 2023, the DeQueen & Eastern received an $11.8 million federal grant for infrastructure improvements, which includes bridge work, so further bridge replacements are likely.

The Little River forms at an elevation of more than 2000 feet in the Ouachita Mountains in southwestern Le Flore County, Oklahoma. The river flows out of the mountains as it heads westward, and then turns to the south around the edge of the mountains. It flows by Wright City and then turns to the southeast and enters Arkansas after about 130 miles. In Arkansas, it flows through Millwood Lake and into the Red River northeast of Texarkana. Parts of the river are popular for canoeing and kayaking, and wildlife areas like the Honobia Creek Wildlife Management Area, Little River National Wildlife Refuge, and the Pond Creek National Wildlife Refuge protect large parts of the river's route.

The Choctaw Lumber Company had a several-mile-long logging spur that headed north in this area during the early days of timber cutting.

6.0   CYPRESS CREEK BRIDGE – This 450-foot-long timber pile trestle crosses a stream named for the large cypress trees that grow along the lower reaches of its channel. The stream forms in the hills in northern McCurtain County and flows southward, entering the Little River less than a mile south of here.

7.3   WRIGHT CITY – The railroad that became the Texas, Oklahoma & Eastern was completed from Valliant to Bismark during November 1909. The railroad's first depot was soon built to handle the lumber business. Several sources state that this community, originally a company town, was created in 1909-1910 when the Dierks brothers incorporated the Choctaw Lumber Company, a subsidiary of the Dierks Lumber & Coal Company, and located its headquarters and sawmill here.

The Oklahoma town was originally named Bismark, using the name of a Nebraska community where the brothers had previously operated a lumber outlet. A post office opened in the Nebraska town in 1868, reportedly named for Otto von Bismarck, a Prussian statesman and politician. The Nebraska town was named Bismarck, while the area was Bismark Township, both in Cuming County.

The Oklahoma post office using the name Bismark opened on March 24, 1910. The First World War made German names unpopular, and many assumed that the town was named after German Chancellor, Otto von Bismarck. Because of this, the community was renamed Wright on September 13, 1918. The name came from William W. Wright, the first soldier from McCurtain County killed during the war. The town and post office took the name Wright City on May 18, 1920, the name still used today.

The original company town reportedly included a stave mill, sawmill, planer, railroad maintenance shops, housing, stores, a bank, hotel, an ice factory, and provision for fire and police protection. There were also churches and a school, supplied by the Dierks company. The hardwood mill and the planing mill that were acquired at De Queen were moved to here after their associated pine mill burned. The railroad also served several agricultural businesses at Wright City, with strawberries being shipped during the 1910s and 1920s.

In 1920, the company's pine mill at Wright City had a capacity of 135,000 feet per ten-hour day. The plant was equipped with two 8-foot Filer & Stowell band mills. It manufactured regular yard stock such as flooring, finished timbers, boards, dimensional lumber, and similar wood shapes. The lath mill could turn out 30,000 lath a day. Supporting the mill was a mill pond with a capacity of about 100,000 feet of logs. The mill also included an ice plant which supplied ice to both Wright City and Broken Bow. By the 1940s, the mill's waste slabs and sawdust were used in furnaces to produce steam for four 1000 kilowatt generators that produced electrical power for the mill and city.

The December 25, 1920, issue of the *American Lumberman* included this photo of the Dierks Lumber & Coal Company mill at Wright City, Oklahoma.

No true count of the number of residents was taken until 1950, and a large census tract that included other area towns was used instead. While no census was conducted at Wright City, it was estimated that the population was less than five hundred during the 1920s. In 1933, a few local cowboys started a rodeo, barbeque, and dance event. It has grown into being the Little Cheyenne, one of the oldest continuous rodeos in Oklahoma.

Wright City was a major hub for the railroad and logging company as a number of logging lines once operated from the sawmill. The town was built to the north of the Texas, Oklahoma & Eastern, and east of the major logging line to the forests north of town. The first official census report stated that the population was 1121 in 1950, and it reported 1161 residents in 1960. As the timber was cut, Dierks decided that it didn't have to maintain the various company towns that it owned, and sold most of its property at Wright City on August 13, 1965.

To organize the community, Wright City was incorporated the following year. Efforts were made to develop a downtown business district. Several facilities such as a community building, medical center, and schools were built. The population stayed slightly above 1000 until the 1980s when it dropped to 836 in the 1990 census. Much of this population drop was due to a reduction of logging and production at the former Dierks plant, operated by Weyerhaeuser since its purchase in 1969. Despite the mill being rebuilt during the 1970s, in late 2005, Weyerhaeuser closed its veneer and plywood plant at Wright City, leaving just the lumber mill here. This plant, described as being the largest sawmill east of the Rocky Mountains, closed in March 2009, and the current population of the town is about 700. A few businesses remain at Wright City, as does the Wright City school system. The Choctaw Nation has a number of offices located at the north end of town along Oklahoma Highway 98.

Parts of the old mill are now used by TLC Rail Services. TLC provides services like railcar cleaning and repair, car storage, transloading, and consulting. The company states that the "facility in Wright City, OK, offers service from the DeQueen & Eastern (DQ & E) Railroad, a Patriot Railroad short line with direct access to Burlington Northern and Santa Fe (BNSF), Union Pacific (UP) and Kansas City Southern (KCS) Railroads. This site is a former forest product production facility with existing rail infrastructure, buildings and 350+ acres with the capacity to hold 250 rail cars on existing track."

While much of the old mill at Wright City has been torn down, this guard house at the main entrance to the mill at Main Street still stands.

One of the tasks handled at Wright City by TLC Rail Services is tank car cleaning. This facility is used to empty and clean tank cars so they can safely be worked on.

In 1999, Wright City was still an important source of wood chips for Weyerhaeuser, as shown by four tracks of cars awaiting loading.

The mainline tracks of today's DeQueen & Eastern still pass by the old chip loading facility at the Dierks sawmill on the east side of Wright City, Oklahoma.

The Railroad at Wright City

At one time, Wright City was almost surrounded by railroad tracks, and it once was the site of a water tank for the company's steam locomotives. The east-west TO&E mainline passed on the south edge of town, and for years some trains were based here, especially with the mill shops capable of maintaining steam locomotives. A small station was built here which served as a telephone station during the early 1900s. It also housed a train register and bulletin books. In 1925, westbound No. 9 would be at Wright City daily except Sunday at 2:55pm. This provided 45 minutes to travel the 7 miles from Golden and handle any business at Wright City. Meanwhile, eastbound No. 10 was scheduled to be here at 5:15pm and take 15 minutes to get to Golden. The railroad's

August 3, 1947, employee timetable showed that there was a 30-car siding, a day telephone office, and water at Wright City.

The December 25, 1920, issue of the *American Lumberman* had a large article about the Dierks Lumber Company. Several pages were used to report on the company's facilities at Wright City, which included this photo of the Wright City Shops. To the left is the front of #375, a 2-8-2 acquired with the initial construction of the Texas, Oklahoma & Eastern.

Milepost 7.3 is located at the wye to the north, a short siding is located on the south side of the main-line, and a spur track heads south into the former Dierks mill complex. The track to the north is on the west side of Wright City and is what is left of the former logging line to Clebit, Oklahoma. This line is currently about 1.5 miles long and crosses Oklahoma Highway 98 at Milepost 0.9. Following the tracks to the west through town is Railroad Street.

Further east, there is a six-track yard south of the mainline between the grade crossing with Main Street (Milepost 7.5) and Cemetery Road (Milepost 8.0). A second spur track heads south from the yard into the mill complex, connecting with a series of tracks that once served the mill pond, log yard, and other parts of the facility. Timetables of the DeQueen & Eastern simply showed the complex as a yard.

Railroad Street runs north-south alongside the Clebit Logging Line on the west side of Wright City, Oklahoma.

The Clebit Logging Line

A number of miles of logging line used to branch out from Wright City as it was for many years the center of area logging. The line was used to harvest much of western and northern McCurtain County. The primary line went north 33 miles to Clebit, Oklahoma, a major Dierks logging camp located southwest of Pickens. Apparently Clebit moved about with the logging activity. It was large enough and stable enough, even before it was located near Pickens, to have a post office that opened on May 7, 1924. The logging camp was named for sawmill foreman John Clebo, but it never was incorporated.

The wye and several miles of the Clebit Logging Line still remain on the west side of Wright City, Oklahoma.

Construction of the Clebit Logging Line began in 1910. The logging railroads that were built by Dierks were designed well, but had lower design standards than the mainline. They had ruling grades of 3%, but short 5-6% grades of about a half-mile-long were allowed. These design standards were even included in the purchase agreements with various steam locomotive manufacturers.

The Clebit Line headed north from Wright City, following Wolf Creek, shown as Rock Creek on many modern maps. It continued north, closely following today's Rodeo Grounds Road and then Merry Highway. The original line was about nine miles long and ended at 9-Mile Camp, also known as Alik-chi #1. This camp operated 1919-1922. Alikchi was considered to be one of the "traveling timber towns" of the Choctaw Lumber Company. The name used for the logging camp, Alikchi, is a Choctaw word that means medical doctor. It had previously been used for the court grounds of the Apukshunnubbee District, established in 1834. Also known as Alik-chi Springs, the town was located about a mile east of today's Ringold. With the passage of the Curtis Act in 1898, which called for the abolition of tribal governments on March 6, 1906, the court was closed and the town slowly went away.

By 1922, the timber was exhausted and timber rights to the north were obtained. The rail route's extension made a series of sharp curves before entering Alikchi #2, located on Terrapin Creek about nine miles further north. This company town also used the name 18-Mile Camp. Here, a 13-mile logging line eventually headed to the northeast, crossed Glover River and followed its East Fork to near Bethel, a small unincorporated community that received a post office on January 24, 1900. Several logging lines branched out from Bethel, including one line that reportedly crossed the Mountain Fork River using a rock pen trestle during the 1930s. Bridges like this were common on logging lines at the time. They consisted of timber frames filled with stones.

18-Mile Camp operated from 1922 until 1929, when the camp was moved east to Camp-in-the-Hole along the branch to Bethel. This camp was also Alikchi #3 as well as Clebit #3 as the two camp operations were combined during the Great Depression. This logging camp lasted until 1933.

In 1933, Clebit #4 was located northeast of Pickens at a place called Clebit-Bethel Camp, served by trucks hauling the timber to the railroad and sawmill at Wright City. The Alikchi camp no longer existed and trucks were being used to haul timber to the railroad, avoiding the construction of temporary logging branches into the woods. Starting in 1938, the main logging spur headed northeast and then northwest 18 miles as it followed the West Fork of Glover River. The main camp was at Pickens, which became Clebit #5 in 1938. This camp remained in operation until 1968.

Clebit and its post office were located at seven different locations as the timbering activity moved northward. The Dierks traveling timber towns consisted of about 200 homes and barracks for 800 workers. Buildings were also supplied for a school, church, water tower, the company store, and even a movie theater. When the towns moved, they were generally loaded onto railcars, but the last few moves were done by truck.

Pickens became the main log terminal for the railroad, and many workers headed into the woods each morning on trucks. As the distance grew, parts of the Clebit Camp moved to the timber cuttings, serving as truck bases. From 1938 until 1944, Clebit #6 (Honobia Camp) was located north of Pickens on a new logging road built to the northwest from Clebit #4. In 1944, this truck camp moved to the northwest of Pickens on a new logging road and became Clebit #7. This camp also used the name Ontuklo Camp. In 1948, this camp closed and all of the facilities were moved back to Pickens (Clebit #5), creating one single Dierks logging camp that served the miles of forests to the north of Wright City.

This photo of a Choctaw Lumber Company logging camp was found in the December 25, 1920, issue of the *American Lumberman*. Note how the buildings could be lifted and placed on railcars to be moved to a new location.

A 1944 report by the National Labor Relations Board involved union activity at the Dierks Lumber & Coal Company, but it also included the logging activity at Clebit. The report stated that the railroad had many different classes of workers at the logging community, including loggers, mechanical workers, and management.

The March 1947 issue of *The Oklahoma State Engineer* had an article about the Oklahoma operations of Dierks Lumber & Coal. Among the details, it included a description of the Clebit Line.

> *The logging, flathead, and truck crews go out into the logging area from the logging camp at Clebit. A logging crew consists of two men whose main equipment consists of a crosscut saw and two double bladed axes. The lumberjacks fell the trees by hand, trim them and top them. If there is a bad crook in the tree, the loggers saw it at the bend. Otherwise, the loggers try to cut the pole into logs varying from twenty to thirty-two feet in length. This practice is*

known as the log-log process because two logs can be cut from one.

Now the logs are ready to be taken to the saw mill to be cut up into lumber. A caterpillar skids the logs, two or three at a time, out of the forest to a loading point alongside one of the company built roads. The logs lay alongside the road until they are picked up by the log trucks. Dierks uses huge Dart trucks having capacities of ninety tons. The trucks have butane engines equipped with eighty gallon fuel tanks. These trucks are never loaded to capacity because there is danger of getting stuck on the mountain roads. These trucks are so heavy that they are never driven on the state or national highways. Logs are loaded onto the trucks mechanically with a tractor and crane. Two men guide the logs as they are put into place on the truck. It takes about fifteen minutes to load a log truck.

The logs are hauled to the railroad right-of-way and unloaded beside the tracks by a caterpillar with a moveable frame attachment. One push by the frame and the truck is unloaded. Logs cut close to the railroad are skidded directly to the right-of-way. The logs along the right-of-way are picked up by a diesel loader, which is a crane with a swinging boom, and loaded on railway cars that are especially designed and equipped to handle logs. The diesel loader runs on rails on top of the flat cars, thus facilitating loading. After a train load of logs, fifteen to twenty cars, has been loaded, the train transports the logs to the saw mill at Wright City.

The 1951 edition of the McAlester, Oklahoma, topographic map (1:250,000 scale), produced by the Corps of Engineers, U.S. Map Service, shows the entire "Dierks Lumber Company" rail line from Wright City to Clebit and Bethel. A U.S. Geological Survey map from 1962 still showed the line, which at that time was identified as an "industrial railroad." Company reports show the line to be Spur #1, while it was locally known as the Clebit Spur. A published report in the *Proceedings of the Oklahoma Academy of Science* (1962) from the same time provided a full description of the Clebit Logging Line.

At present, one private line exists in the state. Dierks Forests, Incorporated, owns and operates this line which is 33 miles long, located entirely within McCurtain County, between Wright City and Clebit. At Wright City, it connects with the Texas, Oklahoma, and Eastern Railway, one of the Dierks owned lines classed as a common carrier.

Construction of this railroad began in 1910 at Wright City and extended to a point nine miles north. This point was the location of Dierks' initial timber exploitation in this area. Timber cutting continued there until 1920 when the timber was exhausted. Timber rights were then acquired and an additional nine-mile extension northward to Alikchi was built. This was the northern terminus until 1938 when additional timber rights were obtained and the line was lengthened northward another 18 miles to Clebit, which is the present northern terminus. In addition, several spurs and branches (tram lines) were constructed. These were in use when mules and wagons transported timber from the cutting area to the tram. They were temporary and could be moved when the timber was exhausted. From 1938-1940, trucks began replacing the team and wagon and the trams were subsequently abandoned.

Rolling stock and equipment consists of a caboose, approximately 45 log and pole cars, and a 900-horsepower diesel-electric locomotive which recently replaced the only steam engine operating in the state. This engine is used only when the diesel is being repaired. The line is standard gauge, with 90-pound rail which results in rather slow movement particularly with heavy loads.

The village of Clebit is actually a Dierks-owned lumber camp and the main focus of timbering operations. Logs are transported in by trucks where they are stockpiled for daily shipment by rail. During rainy weather, the responsibility of supplying timber to the mill at Wright City falls entirely upon the railroad as it is difficult for heavy trucks to negotiate the roads from the cutting area to Clebit and from other areas furnishing timber to the mill.

The Dierks line has one purpose: to transport pine timber, along with a limited quantity of hardwood (predominantly gum, transhipped to Paris, Texas), to Wright City, the location of Dierks only softwood mill in Oklahoma. The line supplies the mill with some 40 percent of the timber utilized. and transports daily (five days per week), an average of 15-20 carloads of timber. This amounts to about 1,600 pine logs resulting in approximately 50,000 board feet of lumber daily. The mill's capacity is 125,000 board feet daily. Other timber required for capacity production is transported by truck from eastern and northeastern locations in McCurtain County and southern Pushmataha County.

During the early 1960s, the logging line supported approximately 100 loggers working in the Clebit area. It also kept the 500 employees at the Wright City mill working. A change was taking place as starting in 1959, Dierks was actually growing more timber than was being harvested. With this strategy, workers believed that the timber business would be here forever.

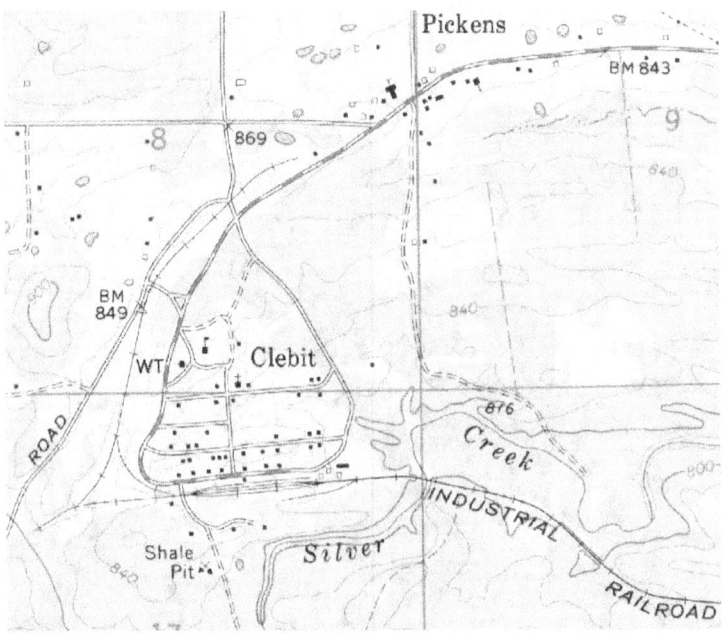

This map from 1972 shows the north end of the Clebit Logging Line at Clebit, Oklahoma. United States Department of the Interior Geological Survey, Clebit Quadrangle – 1972, https://ngmdb.usgs.gov/ht-bin/ tv_browse.pl?id=e91c025d36301aaaada99b02a1b43485

The use of steam on the Clebit Spur ended during the summer of 1963. This steam locomotive, #227 (2-8-2), was later placed on display at Broken Bow, Oklahoma. A diesel locomotive took over the operations as the thought at the time was that the railroad would continue to operate to move the timber harvested near Clebit to the mill at Wright City. However, as roads improved, trucks took over the job of hauling logs. The last log train from Clebit reportedly operated on February 2, 1972. Later that year, Spur #1 was retired, leaving just a short piece of track at Wright City. With the closure of the town, and later the logging activity at Clebit, the post office closed in 1983. Today, little remains of the town and rail yard except a couple of houses, a few foundations, and a number of grades.

The current end of the Clebit Logging Line, also known as Spur #1, is marked by this red sign alongside Oklahoma Highway 98 north of Wright City.

Civilian Conservation Corps Company 2824

Wright City was the home of one of many camps of the Civilian Conservation Corps during the 1930s. Most of Oklahoma's first camps were located in the southeastern part of the state and were designed to handle the sodding or reforestation of local land, often on private property or Indian lands, and to fight forest fires. The camps of this "tree army" contributed an average of $5000 a month to the local economy.

Company 2824 was located one mile northeast of Wright City from August 1935 until August 1938, and was assigned various forestry projects (state forest projects). Because of this, it was designated as Camp SF-68-0. Federal archives reported the following about the camp.

A company of 14 men arrived from Company 1815, located at Pine Valley, and established a camp at Wright City for Company 2824, on August 15, 1935. The new company was enrolled from Bryan and Choctaw Counties, and numbered about 200 boys from families on the relief rolls of the two counties.

The work program of this camp began September 4, 1935. Since this is a heavily timbered country the main objectives have been forest fire prevention, road construction, and civic culture. Hundreds of acres have been cleared of brush and dead trees; tree seedlings planted; bare slopes planted in grass to prevent erosion; dams constructed in natural water storage basins, the water to be used to fight forest fires; 88 miles of trails have been completed; 300-foot steel lookout towers constructed; camping and picnic areas developed; and 100 miles of telephone lines constructed.

8.3 **HORSE HEAD CREEK BRIDGE** – This stream forms to the north in the low hills and flows south to here. A 225-foot-long timber trestle is used to cross this stream, which flows into the Little River a short distance south of here. The railroad has turned to the southeast as it heads towards De Queen.

Not far north of here on Oklahoma Highway 98 is the "Joseph Oklahombi World War I Choctaw Code Talker Bridge." Why the name? Choctaw soldiers were actually the first Native American servicemen to use their native language to relay messages via radio. During World War I, 19 Choctaw servicemen used their language to confuse enemy forces. Four more did the same during World War II. Reportedly, the Choctaw language used in WWI was the only "code" never translated by the German Army. Because of their success, the French government bestowed their highest honor upon the Choctaw Nation for its people's efforts during the war. Joseph Oklahombi was one of these code talkers and he lived along this stream most of his life.

Oklahombi (Choctaw for man-killer or people-killer) served in the Thirty-sixth Infantry Division's Company D, First Battalion, 141st Regiment, Seventy-first Brigade and participated in attacking a German position near St. Etienne, France, on October 8, 1918. He and twenty-three fellow soldiers captured 171 prisoners and several enemy positions. He also helped to rescue a number of wounded men in "No Man's Land." Joseph Oklahombi was awarded the Silver Star with the Victory Ribbon from the

United States, and from Marshal Henri-Philippe Petain he received the Croix de Guerre, one of France's highest honors for gallantry. He lived his entire life in the Wright City area.

The Oklahoma Highway 98 bridge over Horse Head Creek is named for Joseph Oklahombi, once a resident of Wright City. Oklahombi was a World War I code talker and one of the most decorated soldiers from Oklahoma during that war.

11.2 GLOVER RIVER SPUR – The timber along the Glover River was an early target for Dierks Lumber & Coal. The timber further north was logged using the Clebit Logging Line. However, an old grade to the north shows that logging by rail was also done here. Today, a series of logging roads are used to continue to log this area.

Log loading tracks were built and retired as needed all along the railroad. Generally they would last a season or two and then be moved elsewhere, based upon what timber was being cut. To handle this work, the two railroads owned a number of cars to do the work. For example, in 1914, there was pile driver #109 to put in timber trestles, six track laying cars, and 20 boarding cars for the track workers. Much of the track was actually made of panels which could be loaded onto flat cars and moved from place to place. The railroads also handled the loading of logs on some of the lines. To do this, Dierks reported that the railroads had four loaders – #1, #2, #3, and #4.

This photo from *American Lumberman* (December 25, 1920, page 74) shows a log loader preparing a train for the sawmill at Broken Bow, Oklahoma.

11.7 GLOVER RIVER BRIDGE – The railroad has turned back to the east as it crosses the Glover River. The bridge includes a short timber trestle on the west end, then three deck plate girder spans, and then almost 600 feet of timber trestle. In 1926, the Interstate Commerce Commission reported that the steel bridge was 216 feet long.

The Glover River is 33.2 miles long and is a principal tributary of the Little River, which it flows into about a half-mile south of here. While a major waterway, its entire length is in McCurtain County. The Glover River is considered to be a prime spot for fishing and an exciting route for rafting, canoeing and kayaking enthusiasts. It is described as flowing "out of the Ouachita Mountains through a heavily forested area lined by steep bluffs and towering pines." It is still a free-flowing stream with no dams that block its water flow. The river flows through the Three Rivers Wildlife Management Area which is owned by the Weyerhaeuser Company.

14.0 GOLDEN – Golden is an unincorporated community in McCurtain County. The town of Golden was named for James M. Golden, the first postmaster. The date of the founding of the post office was March 13, 1911. This is the fourth Golden post office in Oklahoma. The others were in McClain County (April 9, 1896, to April 21, 1897), Custer County (March 4, 1902, to September 15, 1903), and Beaver County (December 21, 1905, to September 15, 1908). The community has never been more than a few blocks of houses and businesses to the south of the tracks, but the post office is still open.

While Golden was never the site of a large sawmill like nearby Wright City and Broken Bow, there were rates to ship yellow pine and oak lumber, as well as walnut logs, from Golden during the early 1900s. There are some reports about a logging spur track at Golden that was used to harvest the timber on the east side of the Glover River. During the late 1940s, G. W. Thrift operated a small portable pine lumber sawmill at Golden, producing less than 5000 board feet daily.

Despite the town being small, the railroad had a telephone station in a small depot, supporting a logging branch that once headed north from here. In 1925, westbound passenger train No. 9 would be at Golden daily except Sunday at 2:10pm, while eastbound No. 10 was scheduled to be here at 5:30pm. After World War II, a day telephone office remained at Golden due to the number of trains moving on the railroad. There was also a 15-car siding. In 1985, a siding shown as being 4000 feet long and capable of holding 68 freight cars was located at Golden. Today, a long siding still exists on the north side of the mainline.

During the railroad's centennial event on September 30, 2000, locomotive D-28 performed a photo runby at Golden for riders from around the country.

The sidings on the DeQueen & Eastern are seldom used to meet trains, so they are often used to store or interchange freight cars. These cars were spotted on the west end of the Golden Siding in March 2023.

The Golden post office still exists, located south of the tracks at the main grade crossing.

16.0 GRAVEL PIT – The railroad makes a short turn to the south to get around a small hill that was once the location of a gravel pit. The railroad then heads eastward to the grade crossing with Gardenia Road (County Road N4610) at Milepost 17.3 before turning to the northeast to reach Oak Hill, Oklahoma.

The stone from the gravel pit has been used locally by the railroad and for road work and construction. A few of the old road and railroad grades can still be found here.

In this area are a number of small timber trestles and culverts. During the mid-1920s, there was lots of discussion about filling or replacing bridges and culverts along the line. In an interesting statement, C. C. Ray wrote that he did not "believe Mr. Dierks would want us to construct a cement culvert on the D. & E."

The gravel pits at Milepost 16.0 are located at the top of a ridge. This view to the west shows the rolling grades that trains have to fight as they climb the ridge.

18.2   OAK HILL – In 1925, westbound passenger train No. 9 would be at Oak Hill daily except Sunday at 1:55pm, while eastbound No. 10 was scheduled to be here at 5:40pm. Oak Hill was an early station on the railroad, used to support local logging. In 1947, there was a 9-car siding at Oak Hill, but it was gone within a few years.

The name Oak Hill is fairly common in Oklahoma and this one is about five miles west of Broken Bow. The remains of the community of Oak Hill can be found to the north, and includes a scattering of several dozen houses. Oak Hill had a relatively short life as a recognized community. Its post office existed from May 15, 1914, to October 12, 1948. The old Oak Hill school building still stands along the Old Golden Highway north of the tracks. It was built in

1938 by the Works Progress Administration (WPA) using wood frame and clapboard siding. The building is a single story, V-shaped structure, and local labor was used in its construction. The school has been used as a head start facility during the past few years.

Oak Hill is located on a low hill between Courthouse Creek and Lukfata Creek. After the timber was cut, much of the land began to be used for farming, with many crops shipped to market by rail. For example, in 1913, the St. Louis & San Francisco Railroad (Frisco) published new rates for shipping wheat and corn from Oak Hill to Atchison and Leavenworth, Kansas, and St Joseph and Kansas City, Missouri. The railroad also had rates to ship "wagons, farm, and farm trucks" from Ft. Smith, Arkansas, to Oak Hill, as well as Bismark and Broken Bow. Strawberries and cotton were some of the major crops grown here until the 1970s. During the early 1970s, a small independent sawmill operated at Oak Hill. Today, most of the open land is used for grazing and hay production.

As a train heads towards De Queen, it enters the Oak Hill area heading to the northeast and exits it heading to the southeast.

20.1 LUKFATA CREEK BRIDGE – The railroad crosses this stream using a 270-foot-long timber pile trestle.

Lukfata comes from the Choctaw words "lukfi" or "dirt," and "hvta" meaning "light-colored," essentially creating a term for white clay. Lukfata Creek runs though deposits of whitish, light gray clay, picking up the color. The stream was the destination of a number of Choctaw upon their arrival in the new Choctaw Nation as a supply depot was created nearby for Choctaws who settled here. A school opened there in 1833, established by Reverand Loring Williams as a missionary school for native children.

Lukfata Creek was an early landmark of the Choctaw, and the new county that they created was named Bok Tuklo, a Choctaw term that means "two creeks." The two creeks were Lukfata Creek and Yashau Creek. The nearby mountains, considered to be a part of the Kiamichi Mountains, were given the name Bok Tuklo Mountains.

On May 8, 1920, a train was passing over Lukfata Creek when it derailed, killing one and injuring 17, who were taken to the Dierks company hospital at Broken Bow. That is caboose TO&E #0150 on its side. The freight cars involved appear to have been empty logging flats. Courtesy Sevier County Museum, De Queen, AR, Lukfata Creek Derailment.

Lukfata was the destination of a number of Choctaw upon their arrival in the new Choctaw Nation. Little remains of the community except for the Lukfata Cemetery, located north of the tracks about Milepost 21.0.

22.0 HUBER ENGINEERED WOODS SPUR – The railroad again changes direction from heading to the southeast to heading to the northeast. A long spur track curves off to the north that serves the Huber Engineered Woods oriented strand board (OSB) plant, built in 2003. The plant produces board that is used for roof sheathing, subflooring, and other construction needs. The boards are often shipped out by rail, and the glues are often shipped in using railroad tank cars.

In 1883, salesman Joseph Maria Huber arrived in the United States to promote his family's dry colors business. To handle the American market, a plant to produce ink pigments was built, and the J. M. Huber Corporation traces its history to this event. Like many companies, different markets have been entered and exited. Maine timberlands were purchased in 1941, and in 1946 the company began to deal in specialty chemicals. In 1983, Huber opened an oriented strand board (OSB) plant in Easton, Maine, as the start of Huber Engineered Woods (HEW). Today, HEW is one of four parts of the J. M. Huber Corporation.

A spur track heads north at Milepost 22.0 to serve the Huber Engineered Woods plant at Broken Bow, Oklahoma. The plant produces oriented strand board (OSB) used in construction.

22.7 YASHAU CREEK BRIDGE – This timber trestle consists of 16 spans and is 220 feet long. Yashau Creek, along with nearby Lukfata Creek, were the two creeks that the Choctaw Nation's Bok Tuklo County was named for.

This stream flows to the south into Little River and is about 20 miles long. The stream is used to form Broken Bow Lake several miles north of here. The name is believed to have come from a Choctaw word that means "large kettle used for cooking hominy with pork."

To support the Choctaw Lumber Company sawmill at Broken Bow, logging took place along Yashau Creek. To move the lumber, a logging line headed north off of the Texas, Oklahoma & Eastern. From 1927 until 1929, workers lived in a logging camp along the line that was known as Taylor Camp. The camp also was known as Clebit #2 as many of the loggers and much of the equipment moved here when most operations on the Hochatown Logging Line closed in 1927.

23.4 **BROKEN BOW** – By May 1911, the Texas, Oklahoma & Eastern had completed 19 miles of track and was finishing the last four miles to reach what would become the company town of Broken Bow, Oklahoma. According to the Interstate Commerce Commission, this track "was constructed for the carrier by the Choctaw Lumber Company," which built a large sawmill and a stave mill here during the next year. According to *Railway Age* (January 7, 1922), during 1921 the Texas, Oklahoma & Eastern constructed 15.66 miles of railroad from Broken Bow, Oklahoma, to the Arkansas-Oklahoma state line. Because of its location and the sawmill, Broken Bow was an important railroad station that featured a telephone station and a water tower. A logging line also once headed north. In 1925, westbound passenger train No. 9 would be at Broken Bow daily except Sunday at 1:40pm, while eastbound No. 10 was scheduled to be here at 6:45pm.

Broken Bow was an important and busy station on the Texas, Oklahoma & Eastern. While there were many tracks, the siding was only ten cars long in 1947. There was also a day telephone office and water for the steam locomotives. Besides lumber, farm crops like cotton and strawberries were also shipped from the Broken Bow station.

Like many of the towns along the Texas, Oklahoma & Eastern, the railroad passes near the downtown business district, in this case, just to the south.

With the growth of the community, the tracks are now located on the south side of Oklahoma Highway 3 in the center of Broken Bow. In 1985, there was a 1732-foot-long siding that could hold 27 freight cars. Today, there are only several spur tracks south of the mainline and east of Randy Rutherford Boulevard.

PROBLEMS OR EMERGENCIES AT THIS CROSSING REPORT THIS NUMBER 845-170E TO THE DEQUEEN & EASTERN R.R. CALL 1-855-258-4514

While the tracks were built for the Texas, Oklahoma & Eastern, this grade crossing sign at Broken Bow shows that the railroad is the De-Queen & Eastern.

While most of the old tracks are gone, there are a number of reminders about the railroad's earlier days. North of the tracks at 113 W. Martin Luther King (U.S. Highway 70) is the former TO&E depot, restored and used by the Broken Bow Chamber of Commerce. The one-story frame depot was built in 1912 and once stood next to the tracks. The history of the depot states that it was moved to its current location in 1957 from a nearby site.

In 1990, the train station at Broken Bow was looking a bit tired. Note how one end of the building had been modified to store motorcars for the maintenance-of-way department.

The TO&E depot still stands at Broken Bow, Oklahoma, used by the Broken Bow Chamber of Commerce.

Also north of the tracks and east of Park Drive (U.S. Highway 259) can be found Dierks Forests steam locomotive #227 and a wood log car, donated to the City of Broken Bow in 1972 by Weyerhaeuser. Steam locomotive #227 was built by Baldwin in May 1927 and carries construction number 60006. It was built for the Dierks Lumber & Coal Company and arrived at De Queen in June 1927. It initially worked on the logging line between Dierks and Harper Springs Camp. In 1945, it was reassigned to Wright City. With the reorganization of Dierks, it became

145

Dierks Forest #227 in 1954. It was overhauled and repainted in the Wright City shops in September 1962, but made its last run on the Wright City to Clebit line during the summer of 1963.

Dierks #227, a 2-8-2 steam locomotive, sits on display on the west side of the depot in downtown Broken Bow, Oklahoma.

Besides Dierks #227, there is a wooden log car on display at Broken Bow, Oklahoma.

The City of Broken Bow

There were to be several names before the name Broken Bow "took." The first was Con Chito, the name of the Indian village where the downtown section is now located. When the Choctaw Nation moved from Mississippi to their new lands in Indian Territory, the streams and forests around today's Broken Bow attracted a number of the tribe members. A town soon developed in what was Bok Tuklo County of the Apukshunubbee District, one of three administrative super-regions of the Choctaw Nation. The Choctaw Nation still has a major presence here, including their Family Investment Center and several businesses.

As the timber industry moved into the area, loggers began to settle in the community. Among those buying land in the area were Herman and Fred Dierks of the Choctaw Lumber Company. For a short period of time, the community used the name Newtown, and some reports used New Lukfata. However, the Southern Land and Town Site Company, a subsidiary of the Choctaw Lumber Company, developed a new town during June 1911 that it named Broken Bow. The name came from Broken Bow, Nebraska, where the Dierks had previously lived and operated a lumber yard. A public auction was held in September of 1911 to sell most of the 230-acre town, and a post office was established on September 13, 1911. By 1912, the Choctaw Lumber Company had built a large timber processing mill south of the tracks with employee houses to the west, and the town of Broken Bow was developing just north of the Texas, Oklahoma & Eastern Railroad right-of-way.

The Dierks family worked to make Broken Bow a success. They donated land for schools and churches, and a city block that became a city park. A water system was built with a dam on Yashau Creek, and a company hospital provided medical care for the entire town. Electricity was provided to Broken Bow from the sawmill's coal-fired power plant, with the electric system sold to the Public Service Company of Oklahoma in October 1927. The Dierks didn't own everything here with several small, independent sawmills located in the surrounding woods. The Johnson Hotel opened in 1911, but was torn down in 1915 and replaced by the three-story Dell Hotel. The Charles Wesley Hotel opened in 1913, the first brick building was the First National Bank building, and a telephone system soon opened. By 1920, when the population was officially 1983 residents, there were two blocks of businesses north from the tracks along Main Street.

Broken Bow faced an uncertain future when much of the Dierks sawmill burned in early 1925. By July, the company had announced that it would build a new mill. The July 1925 issue of *The Timberman* provided a description of the plans. The double-band mill would be enclosed in a steel building. It would be "completely electrified, with individual motors for each drive, the power to be taken from a transmission line which connects several steam-generating plants owned by the Dierks Lumber & Coal Co. All of the sawmill refuse will be hogged at the mill and shipped to the nearest steam plant. One side of the mill will be built and placed in operation at once, the other side to be built later. Contracts for complete sawmill equipment have been placed with Allis-Chalmers Manufacturing Co., and include an eight-foot type C roller-bearing band mill, roller-bearing No. 2 Allis edger, 17 Allis-Chalmers motor reduction gear sets, and other advanced features."

While the local economy was based upon the logging activities of the various companies owned by the Dierks family, farming also played a role. Both industries were hurt by the depression of the 1930s. To help employ local workers, the National Youth Administration, a division of the Works Project Administration (WPA), built a native stone high school building, now renovated as the Broken Bow Public Library. The WPA also funded the construction of a new city hall, a city hall annex, and the Memorial Stadium.

Because of the mill, Broken Bow survived the Great Depression and reached a population of 2367 in the 1940 census. World War II pulled many workers away as the logging practices became more mechanical, and labor unrest took place in 1947 when the Dierks workers at Wright City, Clebit, and Broken Bow held a two-month-long strike and won an eight-cent-per-hour pay increase. The population of Broken Bow was down to 1838 in the 1950 census, the lowest ever recorded. The year 1955 was a hard one for the community as the workers in the mills and logging camps picketed Dierks for six months before calling off the unsuccessful strike. Despite this, the town saw a steady population growth until the 2000 census, when a record 4230 residents were reported.

In 1969, the operations of Dierks were sold to Weyerhaeuser, and many of the timber and lumber practices began to change. Initially the local employment grew as Weyerhaeuser increased production and instituted a more intensive management of the forests, which includes nearly 900,000 acres in southeast Oklahoma, most of it in the Broken Bow area.

In 1969, the various Dierks properties were sold to Weyerhaeuser. While the sawmill is gone, the timberlands are still operated by Weyerhaeuser, as shown by this sign.

Broken Bow began to diversify its economy in 1970 with the construction of the Lane's Holly Creek Fryers Processing Plant several miles south of Broken Bow. In 1985, the processing plant was sold to Tyson Foods. A Tyson hatchery plant has been built west of town and a feed mill east of town at Craig. Huber Engineered Woods, Pan Pacific Products, and other firms still benefit from the local timber, as does more and more tourism. The Broken Bow Forest Heritage Center features the art work of the creator of Smokey the Bear, Harry Rossoll. The Gardner Mansion and Museum, built in 1884, is known as the historic home of the "Chief of the Choctaws." The Indian Memorial Museum houses numerous artifacts including pre-historic Indian pottery, fossils, Quartz crystal and antique glass. Broken Bow still maintains its own school system and numerous stores, restaurants and hotels can be found along the major roads. A sad part is that where a large sawmill once stood, a shopping center can now be found. The town's population in the 2020 census was 4079.

The Lumber Mills at Broken Bow

Broken Bow was the second logging and mill town created in Oklahoma as the Texas, Oklahoma & Eastern was built eastward. The Choctaw Lumber Company built a pine sawmill that went into service on July 11, 1912, at Broken Bow. They also built a hardwood sawmill in 1914. The pine mill was the primary mill, and a detailed description of the complex was produced in 1920.

The pine mill at Broken Bow has a capacity of 125,000 feet per 10-hour day, and the lath mill has a daily capacity of 25,000. The sawmill is equipped with an 8-foot Filer & Stowell band mill and a 42-inch Wiekes gang. The power for the sawmill is supplied by a 24x30 engine. The powerhouse has eight 150-H.P. horizontal return tubular boilers and a 750-kilowatt turbine generator, the latter supplying electric power for driving the gang in the sawmill and the planing mill machinery besides furnishing light for the plant and for the town of Broken Bow, which has about 2,000 population.

The Broken Bow plant has five kilns, each 20 by 80 feet, affording sufficient capacity for kiln drying the upper grades of stock, the common lumber being piled on the yard to air dry.

The planing mill at Broken Bow has a capacity of 175,000 feet a day. It has complete modern equipment of matchers, molders and resaws for the manufacture of general retail yard stock. The loading platform has capacity for loading twenty cars at one time.

The hardwood mill was smaller, and generally produced lumber for other companies, plus switch ties and car timbers.

The hardwood mill at Broken Bow has capacity for turning out 40,000 feet of hardwood lumber per day of ten hours. It is equipped with a 9-foot Filer & Stowell band mill. This plant manufactures oak and gum lumber principally, with some sycamore, ash and hickory. Most of the stock is cut into lumber for factory purposes. In passing, it may be remarked that most all of the company's output of hardwood lumber is sold to furniture and other woodworking factories, with the exception of the lower grades, which are taken by box factories.

To supply the mills at Broken Bow, the TO&E would haul timber in from surrounding logging operations. There was also a short logging line that followed Yashau Creek to the north.

The Adams Stave Company

Lumber wasn't the only wood product produced along the railroads of Dierks Lumber & Coal. Many of the smaller timbers were manufactured into products like shingles and barrel staves. The first industry located on the Texas, Oklahoma & Eastern at Broken Bow was the Adams Stave Company, which built a large stave mill south of the railroad depot. Some reports state that the mill was owned by J. E. Adams, an associate of the Dierks Brothers, and the company promoted itself for years as "Manufacturers of Tight Barrel Cooperage Stock."

Numerous magazines related to the timber industry reported on the creation of the Adams Stave Company. The August 1911 issue of *Packages* had probably the most detailed report about the start of the firm.

> *J. A. Adams, Sons, Amity, Ark., manufacturers of tight barrel staves, have dissolved, and a new company formed with the title of Adams Stave Co., with headquarters at Lukfata, Ok., and paid up capital of $50,000. The stockholders are as follows: Herman Dierks, president, Kansas City, Mo.; John E. Adams, vice president, Lukfata, Ok.; H. L. Dierks, secretary, Kansas City, Mo.; Fred Runyan, treasurer, Lukfata, Ok. The Adams company has erected a new plant at Lukfata.*

While this report used the town name of Lukfata, the name was used for a rural community that was located immediately west of Broken Bow. Located on the east bank of Lukfata Creek, the area was a planned mill site for the Choctaw Lumber Company. A construction office was set up under the charge of James Monroe Campbell. Campbell had earlier been president of the Arkansas & Choctaw Construction Company, which built the St. Louis & San Francisco line through Valliant. Today, the community where the company built its facilities is Broken Bow, and there are few reminders of this early Choctaw community except for the Lukfata Cemetery and the Lukfata Public School. Other reports used Idabel and "Bismarck" as the location of the company. The stave mill was built in 1911 and moved to Dierks, Arkansas, in 1918.

While the Dierks were part of the stave business, that didn't stop the Adams Stave Company from filing rate complaints against the Texas, Oklahoma & Eastern Railroad. The company shipped whiskey and oil staves, made from gum and oak, across the country. For example, in 1915, the stave firm fought the rates being paid for staves moving to locations like Fresno and San Francisco, California, and Chicago Heights, Illinois. Over a few years, the Interstate Commerce Commission declared that the rates to various other points in the United States were "found unreasonable to the extent that they exceed by more than 2 cents per 100 lb. the rates from Valliant to the same destinations."

25.2 YANUBBEE CREEK BRIDGE – Heading east from Broken Bow, the railroad turns first to the northeast at Yanubbee Creek, and then to the southeast at Peavey Crossing Road (Milepost 26.8), and then back to the northeast at Oak Grove Road (Milepost 28.4) to avoid a series of low hills.

Yanubbee Creek, sometimes spelled Yanubbe Creek, forms about 10 miles north of Broken Bow from several small streams and flows southwards into Crooked Creek. The railroad crosses it here using a 270-foot-long, 19-span timber pile trestle, with several bents over the main channel of the stream having cement footings due to past washouts. The term Yanubbee is a name derived from the Choctaw language and means ironwood.

This curved timber trestle crosses Yanubbee Creek a short distance east of Broken Bow, Oklahoma. Note the concrete footings designed to support the bridge during times of flooding.

28.4 OAK GROVE – Oak Grove was never really a station stop for the Texas, Oklahoma & Eastern, but there is a small community with several churches and cemeteries to the south. The location can be found where Oak Grove Road crosses the tracks. Here, eastbound trains change from heading southeast to northeast.

30.4 CRAIG – At Milepost 30.4 there is a wye to the south that connects to the Craig Spur, built in 1960, with the name and billing location approved as a new station by the Interstate Commerce Commission on April 15, 1960. The Craig Spur headed south to Milepost 1.6 at the Weyerhaeuser Craig Plant that manufactured medium density fiberboard, a panel of compressed wood fiber and resin that was used primarily for furniture. The plant also produced insulated board used in building construction. The first part of the fiberboard plant was built in 1971, and at its peak, the plant employed more than 200 workers. On January 30, 1990, Weyerhaeuser announced that it would close the plant due to market conditions and competitive pressures. Pan Pacific Products at Broken Bow later purchased the equipment from the Weyerhaeuser Craig Plant and began developing new product lines made from medium density fiberboard. While the Craig Plant is gone, Bell Lumber & Pole has used some of the property. Bell Lumber began in 1909 when M. J. Bell started a sawmill in northern Wisconsin. It became the Bell Lumber Company in 1909 and then Bell Lumber & Pole Company in 1930. In 2015, the company built a pole production facility here. By late 2023, construction was underway on an expanded facility and carloads of poles could be seen at the plant. For the railroad, there is a small railyard just north of the Bell Lumber complex.

The real active shipper on the spur track is Tyson's Craig Feed Mill at Milepost 1.0, which supplies many of the area poultry farms. Tyson Foods is big, producing 20% of the chicken, beef, and pork in the United States.

The pole plant of Bell Lumber & Pole uses the property where the Weyerhaeuser Craig Plant once manufactured medium density fiberboard.

Tyson Foods started in 1931 when John W. Tyson moved to Springdale, Arkansas, and to feed his family, began buying chickens locally and selling them across the Midwest. The business grew rapidly during World War II as poultry was one of the few foods not rationed, and Tyson moved into chicken production. The company was incorporated in 1947 as Tyson Feed and Hatchery, Inc. During the late 1950s, the company built its first processing plant, meaning that it raised, processed and sold poultry, one of the first firms to control the entire process.

In 1963, Tyson's Foods went public, allowing it to continue to expand. The name became Tyson Foods in 1972, and other product lines were added throughout the 1980s. By 1990, Tyson Foods was the world's largest fully-integrated producer, processor, and marketer of poultry-based food products, and was quickly expanding its international market. Thanks to further expansion and several acquisitions, Tyson became the world's largest processor and marketer of chicken, beef, and pork by 2001. Since then, the company has continued to expand

and the product names on the side of their trailers will surprise almost anyone.

On November 4, 2022, the feed mill and a number of area poultry farms were damaged or destroyed by a large tornado. Months later, repairs were still being conducted on the feed mill.

This sign marks the entrance to the Tyson Feed Mill at Craig, at times a significant shipper on the DeQueen & Eastern Railroad.

The Craig Feed Mill is busy enough to warrant the use of Tyson locomotive #13873. This locomotive was manufactured in 1950 as Illinois Central #9422, an SW7. It was later rebuilt into an SW14, Illinois Central #1415.

Tyson's Craig Feed Mill stands one mile south of the Craig Wye, and serves a series of large poultry farms in the area.

John McDaniel Craig was a manager with Dierks who started in the industry as a water carrier for a sawmill. In 1909, he began working in the offices at De Queen, and within a few years was the assistant manager of the Idabel, Oklahoma, office. He became manager of the office by 1913. Craig was involved with numerous businesses in the region and served as vice president of the First National Bank of Broken Bow. A relative of his, Elizabeth Craig, married Herbert Dierks, the son of Hans Dierks. John Craig passed away on November 25, 1959, after 51 years with Dierks, with his last title being Manager of the Dierks Land Department in Oklahoma.

North of the tracks at the intersection of U.S. Highway 70 and Craig Road was once a small community known as Tiner, named for the local school house. The small one-room building, one of the few remaining in Oklahoma, was constructed in 1921 and was named for the builder, Walter Tiner. It measures approximately 27 feet wide by 35 feet long and was used to house the first through the eighth grades. The school closed in 1938 but the building has survived, serving other purposes. It was added to the National Register of Historic Places on November 21, 1980.

This is the Tiner School House, located north of the tracks at Craig, Oklahoma. This small school building served the local community until 1938, and is today listed on the National Register of Historic Places.

30.9 MOUNTAIN FORK RIVER BRIDGE – This series of steel deck plate girder spans, set on concrete piers, replaced a set of three through truss spans during the early 2000s. The bridge was shown to measure 545 feet long when the Interstate Commerce Commission investigated the railroad. When the plans for the Texas, Oklahoma & Eastern were announced, the Mountain Fork River was the original destination. Eventually, the river was bridged to allow the line to be completed to De Queen, Arkansas, with November of 1917 as the cited date of the opening of the bridge.

The Mountain Fork River, also known as the Mountain Fork of the Little River, is a 98-mile-long stream that is a principal tributary of Oklahoma's Little River. The river, despite being broken into the Upper and Lower courses by the Broken Bow Lake, is hailed as the best whitewater stream in Oklahoma. The river forms in the Ouachita Mountains in Le Flore County, Oklahoma, and flows into Arkansas before turning back to the southwest to Broken Bow Lake. That part of the river is described as having 32 miles of "Class I and II rapids, clear water, fishing for Smallmouth bass and other species, and excellent scenery with pine forests covering the hills and bluffs along the river's course."

The lower Mountain Fork River is a short, but very exciting stream that offers both flat water and whitewater below Broken Bow dam. The lake makes this 19-mile part of the river the most consistently flowing stream in Oklahoma. Below the dam, Rainbow and Brown Trout are stocked regularly throughout the year. Further down the river, Bald Cypress trees line and, in some places, grow in the river. From the TO&E bridge, it is only nine miles downstream to the Little River.

To log the timber along the Mountain Fork River, the Choctaw Lumber Company and the Texas, Oklahoma & Eastern had several short spur tracks along the stream. In October 1921, the railroad was looking to establish a gravel pit north of Eagletown near the Mountain Fork River. Later, there was an important logging line that headed north just east of the Mountain Fork River. This line served the Eagletown Camp, a logging camp operated by Choctaw Lumber from 1924 until 1932.

The original through truss bridge over the Mountain Fork River is shown in this photo taken from a hirail truck in 1999.

During the railroad's centennial event on September 30, 2000, locomotive D-27 performed a photo runby at the Mountain Fork River bridge. Note that the through truss spans still stood at that time.

The new bridge over the Mountain Fork River uses specially notched deck plate girder spans so they can fit on the old concrete piers that once supported through truss spans. This view is from the boat launch area under the new U.S. Highway 70 bridge, located to the north of the tracks.

32.3 MARTIN MARIETTA BROKEN BOW SAND & GRAVEL WYE – The wye to the south allows trains to reach an aggregate loader and a 6-track rail yard. Throughout this area are a series of active and retired pits from mining sand and gravel. Currently, Martin Marietta operates this large facility, one of more than 500 the company works. The company advertises this mine as producing aggregates, an "engineered, granular material consisting of crushed stone and sand and gravel, manufactured to specific sizes, grades and chemistry for use primarily in construction applications."

According to the *2018 Oklahoma State Rail Plan*, Oklahoma ranks third in originating crushed stone, sand, and gravel products that move by rail, and ranks eighth for rail movements of the same products that terminate in the state.

This sign marks the highway entrance into the Martin Marietta Broken Bow Sand & Gravel facility, a short distance west of Eagletown, Oklahoma.

32.7 LUKSUKLO CREEK BRIDGE – This stream, sometimes spelled Liksuklo, forms in the hills less than ten miles to the north. In that area, it is often known as Lick Creek. It then flows to the south and enters the Mountain Fork River a mile to the south. The stream is easy to find because of the 450-foot-long timber trestle used by the railroad.

North of the tracks on U.S. Highway 70 is the "Calvin Wilson World War I Choctaw Code Talker Bridge." This is another highway bridge that honors one of the Choctaw soldiers who used their language to defeat the German army during the First World War. Calvin, misspelled in military records as "Cabin," was born at Eagletown on June 25, 1894. He was a member of the 142nd Infantry, Company E.

CALVIN WILSON
WWI CHOCTAW CODE TALKER
BRIDGE

The U.S. Highway 70 bridge over Luksuklo Creek is named in honor of Calvin Wilson, a native Choctaw from Eagletown who served as a code talker in the 142nd Infantry during World War I.

33.3 EAGLETOWN – The milepost historically used for Eagletown is at the SW Second Street grade crossing at the west end of town. Eagletown was a newer station on the TO&E, created when the railroad completed its line between Broken Bow and De Queen, and then the logging company built a line northward to reach the area's timber. The railroad built a depot 2.5 miles southeast of the Mountain Fork River bridge, a short distance away from the original Eagletown (Eagle Town) community. The depot was a station that could issue train orders and handle freight and passenger business as it was an official telephone station. In 1925, westbound passenger train No. 9 would be at Eagletown daily except Sunday at 12:50pm, while eastbound No. 10 was scheduled to be here at 7:15pm. For many years, there was a 10-car siding. The tracks once located at Eagletown slowly went away and in 1985 there was a short 986-foot-long track that could hold 14 cars. Today, no side tracks exist.

Heading towards De Queen, the railroad turns to the northeast until Milepost 35.5, where it turns to the southeast. At Milepost 37.5, the tracks curve again, heading to the east. Looking at a map, the tracks of the Texas, Oklahoma & Eastern between Broken Bow and Milepost 37.5 look like a large saw blade. This is appropriate as the area is covered with timber plantations.

The History of Eagletown

Welcome to Miller County, Arkansas, or at least it was until the 1820s when it became a part of the lands assigned to Indian Territory. White settlers had moved into the area during the first several decades of the 1800s and were forced to move as the region was assigned to the Choctaw Nation. The first Choctaw arrivals found cleared fields and log cabins, but little food, fish or game to survive on. Instead, the U.S. Army established a supply point to distribute rations several miles east of the Mountain Fork River. A reported 852 tribal members were receiving rations here in April 1832, and 1500 by 1834.

Because many of the first arrivals came here, and because of the supply depot, a town was almost immediately created on the east side of the Mountain Fork River, the first permanent Choctaw settlement in the Indian Territory. The residents called the location "osi yamaha," often spelled Osi Tamaha. The term was translated to mean Eagle, but the reason cannot be agreed upon. One story says that it was named for the many eagles that nested in nearby swamps along the Mountain Fork River. However, another story says that it was named as a joke by the Choctaws. This story says that Indians would state that they were going to see the eagle whenever they had a meeting with the U.S. Army or the Indian agent due to the use of the eagle as the United States symbol.

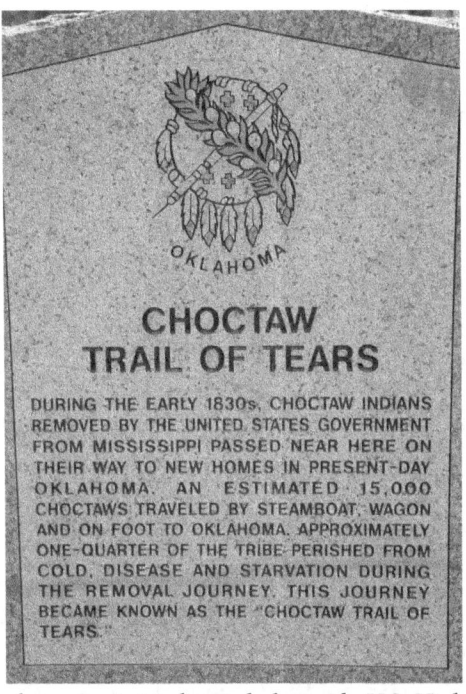

This historical monument is located alongside U.S. Highway 70, and tells the story of the Choctaw Trail of Tears, which closely followed the future route of the Texas, Oklahoma & Eastern.

Because this was one of the supply points for the arriving Choctaw, several of its leaders settled here. Chief Peter Pitchlynn was a leader in the removal of the Choctaw, having helped to negotiate the Treaty of Dancing Rabbit Creek in 1830. He had been educated at several schools, including the University of Nashville. While a planter at Eagletown, he helped create the Choctaw national educational system, worked on creating the Choctaw Constitution, was a principal chief (1864-1866), and served as a Choctaw representative in Washington, D.C., for many years. Chief George Hudson was educated back east, worked as a wheelwright, and practiced law. He arrived here in 1832 and lived on the west bank of the Mountain Fork River. He was chair of the Choctaw Constitution Convention in 1860 and served as principal chief 1860-1862.

Religion was important to the Choctaw, and a number of white missionaries were invited to join them in Indian Territory. In 1832, Reverend Loring S. Williams was sent by the American Board of Commissioners for Foreign Missions to establish a mission school and church. He located his school and community on the west bank of the Mountain Fork River, naming it Bethabara (Hebrew for "a crossing"), evidently referring to the local crossing of the Mountain Fork. Williams also established the Eagle Town post office on July 1, 1834. In 1836, the Stockbridge Mission was established nearby. Here, Cyrus Byington compiled the *Dictionary of the Choctaw Language*. Many of these missions opened and closed, and the town changed locations a number of times, however, it has always stayed close to the river. One cause of the movement was the Military Trace, a military road between Fort Towson and government posts in Arkansas. This road changed its route based upon the best river ford, and many travelers stopped to resupply at Eagle Town.

In 1850, the Choctaw Nation created and passed its constitution and Eagle County, Apukshunnubbee District, Choctaw Nation was established. The existing Eagle Town became the "courtground" for Eagle County, and later a pine log courthouse was built. One of the local leaders was Jefferson Gardner, a Choctaw trader who operated a series of general stores. He built a large home on the west side of the Mountain Fork River that is now listed on the National Register of Historic Places. Gardner became an elected principal chief of the Choctaw Nation (1894-1896), but later lost his fortune.

On December 16, 1892, the town's name was changed to Eagletown. On November 16, 1907, Indian Territory and Oklahoma Territory merged to become the State of Oklahoma, the 46th state. With the change, Eagle County was dissolved and replaced by McCurtain County, and Eagletown was no longer a county seat. Another change happened when the Texas, Oklahoma & Eastern built through the area in 1920 and constructed a depot nearby. Most of the businesses and residents moved to the depot area, creating the current site of Eagletown.

Farming had always been a primary business for many area settlers, but timber became important with the arrival of the railroad. The Choctaw Lumber Company established a logging camp at Eagletown with housing and other services for their workers and families. In 1921, H. L. Dierks had a survey conducted, and a plat created, for a 46.26-acre town as a part of the logging camp at Eagletown. On December 20, 1921, the Southern Land & Townsite Company of Broken Bow, Oklahoma, held a sale of residential and business lots at Eagletown. While never a Dierks mill town, at least one Choctaw Lumber logging line left the TO&E mainline here. Today, Eagletown is an unincorporated community with a population of about 500. A school, post office, a few businesses, and a number of homes can be found scattered throughout the townsite to the north of the tracks.

EAGLETOWN, OKLAHOMA

New Townsite Sale

OF

BUSINESS AND RESIDENCE LOTS

ON

Tuesday, Dec. 20, 1921

All Lots Sold on Liberal Terms

Eagletown is Located on the T.O. & E. Ry beteen Valliant,Okla. and DeQueen, Ark. 10 miles east of Broken Bow, Okla.

On December 20, 1921, a sale of the lots in the new Eagletown was held. Ads like this one were found in newspapers across the country promoting the event. *The Little River News*. Ashdown, AR, Dec. 17 1921. Retrieved from the Library of Congress https://www.loc.gov/item/sn90050316/1921-12-17/ed-1/.

Weyerhaeuser still owns timberlands around Eagletown and maintains an office to manage their operations.

The Hochatown Logging Line

During the 1920s and 1930s, the Choctaw Lumber Company (Dierks) had a logging line heading north out of Eagletown that reached as far as Hochatown, about 10 miles away. The lumber company established a lumber camp near Hochatown, and it was large enough to have its own commissary. There were several shorter spur tracks off of the Hochatown Logging Line, at least one of which headed east and crossed into the very northwest corner of Sevier County, Arkansas.

Probably the best known branch off the Hochatown Logging Line was the Winship Branch. The name Winship can still be found in the area thanks to the Winship Prairie, Old Winship Road, and Winship Prairie Road. This branch is still known thanks to many family stories about the Winship Branch Washout that caused a train wreck in 1929.

Hochatown was originally settled by twelve Choctaw families during the 1880s. These early inhabitants planted a few crops and spent a great deal of time hunting and trapping. The community was located on the east bank of the Mountain Fork River, and the town's name came from the Choctaw word for river, "hvcha," giving it the basic meaning of river town. A post office opened there in 1894. Some histories state that the post office arrived with the construction of the logging camp and railroad, but the railroad didn't reach Eagletown until more than 20 years later after the Mountain Fork River bridge opened during November 1917.

As the lumber company built northward from Eagletown, one of the first logging camps established was Clebit Camp, a camp that moved seven times before finishing up near Pickens on the line north of Wright City. Because Clebit Camp moved to a variety of places, Clebit Camp also was known as Clebit #1, which officially operated 1924-1927. By the 1930s, the timber was cut in the area and the Dierks operations were mostly replaced by a small private sawmill and stave mill. The logging railroad was soon removed and the logging camp structures were moved elsewhere.

During the 1930s, the Eagletown Civilian Conservation Corps (CCC) camp was located near Tablerville, about 9 miles north of Eagletown. This was where the original Dierks Clebit #1 lumber camp operated, providing housing for timberworkers from the Choctaw Lumber Company. Clebit #1 is generally considered to be the first location of what were known as the "traveling timber towns" of McCurtain County.

Logging was quickly replaced by farming, and Hochatown gained the title of "Moonshine Capital of Oklahoma," given by a federal revenue agent during a trial in federal court in Muskogee. Apparently the corn and clear water from the river were being put to good use. After the lumber company left, a general store and a school opened to replace the facilities owned by Dierks, but the town moved several miles to the west to get on higher ground during the 1960s. This was necessary due to the construction of the Broken Bow Dam on the Mountain Fork River. The post office closed in 1963 and the final family left the community in 1966. The old Hochatown is now more than 40 feet below the waters of Broken Bow Lake.

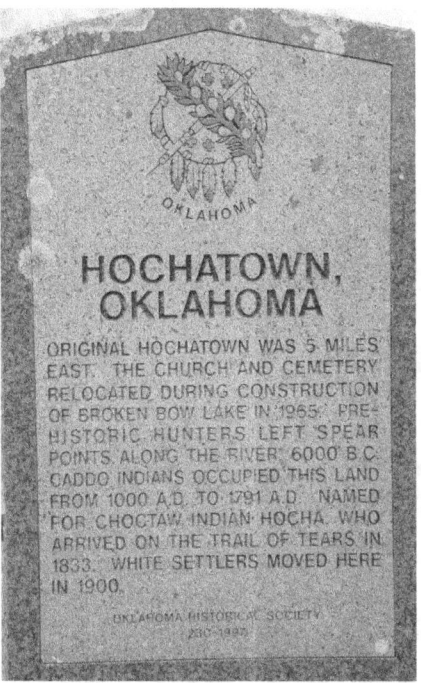

This historical marker was erected in Hochatown by the Oklahoma Historical Society in 1997.

In 1935, the Choctaw Lumber Company sold 1200 acres of cut-over land to a group of local citizens from Broken Bow and Idabel. These citizens paid $1808 for the land to help start a state park along the Mountain Fork River. The land was quickly deeded to the State of Oklahoma for the creation of Beavers Bend State Park. During August 1935, Company 2815 of the Civilian Conservation Corps (CCC) moved to the site and began building various park facilities. Many of these buildings were designed by Herbert Maier and his team of designers and engineers, who also designed structures at Yellowstone, Grand Canyon and Yosemite National Parks. Today, the park's Heritage Center features a number of displays about the area, including an entire room about logging and Dierks Lumber & Coal.

Beavers Bend State Park, located north of Broken Bow, was built on former Dierks timberlands. Its Heritage Center features a large display about Dierks Lumber & Coal and its logging activities.

Until a few years ago, the new Hochatown was simply a small lake community, with an official population of 242 in the 2020 census. However, it has recently been discovered and now features a large casino and hotel, around 2500 cabins, and numerous stores and restaurants. The population is still small, but it has become a resort town, especially used by Texans as this is the first part of the Ouachita Mountains that they reach when heading north. The area is so popular that a number of developments are underway that include hundreds of cabins selling for $500,000 or more. To protect the community from outside control, Hochatown residents voted to incorporate the community on November 8, 2022. The McCurtain County Commissioners approved the articles of incorporation on November 28, 2022, and the first meeting of the town trustees was held on January 10, 2023.

37.0 BUCK CREEK BRIDGE – Buck Creek is another stream that forms in the hills to the north and then flows southward into the Little River. In this case, the stream flows to the southeast and enters the Little River less than a mile inside of Arkansas. The railroad crosses Buck Creek using a 140-foot-long timber pile trestle.

37.6 THIRTY EIGHT – For years, a short 1776-foot-long siding was located at the grade crossing with County Road D4810. The siding took the name of the closest milepost on the railroad, thus Thirty Eight. At a length of about 28 freight cars, it was designed to handle interchange between the TO&E and DQ&E, to pass trains, and it could be used for log loading when the nearby forests were being harvested. This track is now gone.

39.9 STATE LINE – The border between Oklahoma and Arkansas can be found at the grade crossing with West Line Road. A survey bench mark shows that this location is at an elevation of 336 feet. To the west is **Oklahoma**, once known as Indian Territory (1834-1907), and later partly as Oklahoma Territory (1890-1907). This area used to be Miller County of Arkansas Territory, which was created on April 1, 1820. Miller County was big, and actually included parts of Arkansas (Little River, Polk and Sevier counties), Texas (Bowie, Cass, Delta, Fannin, Franklin, Hopkins, Hunt, Lamar, Morris, Red River and Titus counties), and Oklahoma (Choctaw, Latimer, LeFlore, McCurtain and Pushmataha counties).

The county stretched west until November 15, 1824, when the very western part of the territory was removed. The rest of the land west of today's Arkansas-Oklahoma border was removed on May 6, 1828, and the property in Texas was claimed by that new Republic in 1836. The original county was named for James Miller, the first governor of the Arkansas Territory.

Oklahoma means "red people" in the Choctaw language, and the name was decided during an 1866 meeting between federal officials and leaders of the five Indian nations who had been moved there. During the late 1800s, the western part of what became Oklahoma was the Oklahoma Territory, while the eastern part was Indian Territory. The two merged and became the 46th state on November 16, 1907. It is the 20th largest state and the 28th most populated, with about four million residents, with two-thirds of Oklahomans living in the Oklahoma City (the state capital) and Tulsa metropolitan areas. The state is known as "The Sooner State" due to the number of white settlers who staked their land claims out before the official opening date in the western Oklahoma Territory. The Railroad Act of 1886 opened the way for railroad construction across Indian Territory. The builders of the various railroads took advantage of this Act to build across the state, in what was actually a relatively late burst of railroad activity.

The track west to Valliant is all in **McCurtain County**. McCurtain County replaced Eagle County in the area and was named for a prominent Choctaw family, three of whom had served as principal chiefs of the tribe. At the time of its creation, the population was 13,198 residents. The new county was located in the extreme southeastern corner of the state, and Idabel became its county seat. It is the third-largest county in Oklahoma and basically covers the territory between the foothills of the Ouachita Mountains south to the Red River. The county includes land that was some of the first settled with the creation of the Choctaw Nation within Indian Territory, but its population grew quickly with the timber boom of the 1910s and 1920s, reaching 37,906 in 1920. The population peaked at 43,000 residents in 1950 and has slowly declined since then, with farming and timber dominating the county. McCurtain County had a population of 30,814 in the 2020 census.

To the east is Arkansas and Sevier County. The Territory of **Arkansas** was admitted to the Union as the 25th state on June 15, 1836. It is the 29th largest state, and the 32nd most populated. This part of the state is the Ouachita Mountains. It is part of the interior highlands region, the only major mountainous region between the Rocky Mountains and the Appalachian Mountains. Arkansas is also the only state where diamonds are mined, and you can go mine them yourself at the Crater of Diamonds State Park. The former nickname of the state was the Land of Opportunity, but it now uses The Natural State. Little Rock, located near the center of Arkansas, is the capital and largest city in the state.

Sevier County is located in southwest Arkansas and borders the state of Oklahoma. The Little River, crossed by the TO&E west of here, forms the southern boundary of the county, while the Saline River borders the east side. Settlement began about 1810, and when the Choctaw started moving out of Mississippi in 1820, the tribe received land in southwest Arkansas. In 1825, they agreed to move to Indian Territory, but some stayed or worked in Sevier County.

Sevier County was created on October 17, 1828, named for Ambrose Sevier, U.S. Senator from Arkansas. The county has since been cut up to create other counties. The first county seat was Paraclifta, but was moved to Lockesburg in 1871 after the Lockes family donated land for the community. It finally moved to De Queen in 1905. The county's economy has historically been based upon agriculture – corn, cotton, strawberries, cucumbers, sweet potatoes, watermelons, peanuts, peaches, and cantaloupes. Timber later became the most important industry. About seventy percent of the county is still timberland, and the current population is about 17,000 residents.

Things don't always go right on the railroad. In early 2023, these grain cars were still laying on their sides near the Westline Road grade crossing.

Westline Road crosses the railroad at Milepost 39.9, right at the state line between Oklahoma and Arkansas. The railroad station of West Line is a short distance to the east, and the West Line Cemetery is about a mile to the southeast.

40.4 WEST LINE – West Line has an interesting reason to exist. This is where the two railroads, the DeQueen & Eastern and the Texas, Oklahoma & Eastern, connected starting on January 5, 1921. The location is east of the Arkansas/Oklahoma border and there is a short siding to the south that is 939 feet long and can hold about 13 freight cars. During the first few decades of the railroad's existence, West Line was an official passenger train stop. In 1925, westbound No. 9 would be at West Line daily except Sunday at 12:30pm, while eastbound No. 10 was scheduled to be here at 7:30pm. In 1947, the railroad's timetable showed the station's name as Westline, and the siding as being ten cars long.

West Line was once a small logging community, and the West Line Cemetery is located a mile to the south on West Line Road, which is County Road 1. The cemetery is still active, and graves date back to as early as 1873. A post office was also located here, but only during 1922-1927. A few houses and a series of poultry houses help mark the location of West Line, as does Old Schoolhouse Drive.

Just east of the siding, the railroad crosses Two-mile Creek on a 100-foot-long bridge. A number of small streams flow off the low hills in the area and the railroad uses a series of timber trestles to cross them.

40.9 ROCK CREEK BRIDGE – Look for the 300-foot-long timber pile trestle. Rock Creek forms on the east side of Sage Mountain, about five miles east of Broken Bow Lake in Oklahoma. It flows to the southeast into Arkansas, about five miles north of here. About five miles south of the railroad, Rock Creek flows into the Rolling Fork River.

East of the logging road grade crossing at Milepost 41.4 are several more timber pile trestles, many 200 feet or more long. These all allow high water to flow south during flood conditions.

A January 1921 report stated that the new track through the Rolling Fork bottoms was two feet below the high water mark of August 1915. Much of this was due to the settling of the grade on the saturated bottomland. Because of this, the railroad made plans to widen the grade so it could be raised and ballasted.

42.9 ROLLING FORK RIVER BRIDGE – The Rolling Fork River is one of the principal tributaries of the Little River. The river is 55 miles long and forms in the Ouachita Mountains near Hatton, Arkansas, and flows south to here and then on to the Little River. The river is dammed north of De Queen to form De Queen Lake (also spelled DeQueen Lake and Dequeen Lake in various government documents), a U.S. Army Corps of Engineers project completed in 1977. The lake is heavily used for recreation, including fishing, boating, camping, picnicking, hiking and hunting.

To finally connect the Texas, Oklahoma & Eastern with the DeQueen & Eastern, grading work in the Rolling Fork River bottoms began by November 1918. Because of its isolated location, a construction camp was established in the area. The April 17, 1919, issue of *Manufacturers Record* reported on the construction. "Grade is 50 per cent. complete on 9-mi. extension De Queen & Eastern Rwy., from De Queen to the Arkansas-Oklahoma boundary line. J. C. Leathers and Jim Howell of De Queen have contracts. One steel bridge of 100 feet span to be let. Also 15 mi. of track to be laid."

A report on the front page of the *De Queen Bee* (September 17, 1920) reported that the TO&E would reach De Queen by February 1, 1921, if there was favorable weather. One of the delays cited was installing the steel girders over the Rolling Fork River, plus the numerous timber pile trestles in the Rolling Fork bottoms. This delay involving the construction of the bridge over the Rolling Fork River is supported by several DeQueen & Eastern reports from November 1920 which state that the company is "waiting on girders for Rolling Fork River bridge."

The steel rails were laid from Westline to De Queen in 1920. The last spike was driven by Matthew F. Allen, who was the Second Vice-President of both the DeQueen & Eastern and the Texas, Oklahoma & Eastern. The official time and date was 4:23pm on January 5, 1921.

The DeQueen & Eastern Railroad bridge consists of five deck plate girder spans over the main channel, plus a long series of timber trestles on the west end. The entire bridge is 600 feet long.

44.1 ROLLING FORK – For a short period of time, there was a spur track near here known as Rolling Fork, Arkansas. Rates for shipments of products like cement and timber were in effect by 1924. In 1934, six carloads of cull peaches in bulk were shipped from here between July 30th and August 3rd. The six shipments aggregated 164,000 pounds and averaged 27,333 pounds per carload. They moved over the DeQueen & Eastern Railroad Company to De Queen and then the Kansas City Southern Railway Company to Siloam Springs, Arkansas. The shipper, Robinson Canning Company, later complained that the rates were "unreasonable and unduly prejudicial." After a series of hearings, the Interstate Commerce Commission found that the rates were not shown to have been unreasonable.

The location was still shown in the railroad's timetable in 1947. However, there was no siding.

On July 24, 1999, Union Pacific 7078 is pulling an empty coal train eastbound towards De Queen. These coal trains served the Western Farmers Electric Cooperative Hugo Plant and operated over the De-Queen & Eastern for several years.

45.1 **WEST END DE QUEEN YARD LIMITS** – A great deal of switching takes place at De Queen. Because of this, the tracks between Mileposts 45.1 and 54.0 are protected by yard limits. From here to the west at Milepost 2.0, the railroad uses Track Warrant Control to authorize train movements.

This switch, located at the Dog Town Road crossing, is the west end of the Process City complex. The siding is often used to hold cars until they are needed by trains working the De Queen yards.

45.7 **PROCESS CITY** – There are a series of tracks in this area, used over the years for several different facilities. The last one was a wood treatment plant built by Dierks in 1948. The plant for years treated landscape timbers, utility poles, fence posts, barn poles, lumber, and railroad ties using a 110-foot-long and 96-inch-diameter cylinder. So much wood was treated here that the plant added four hundred railroad cars of freight a month to the railroad. The plant used Pentachlorophenol (PCP, or penta), an industrial wood preservative used since 1936. In 1957, it was reported that the modern wood preserving plant at Process City treated millions of fence posts with creosote and penta annually. In 2004, Weyerhaeuser discontinued the wood treatment operations and began decommissioning the plant.

The complex begins at Milepost 45.5, just east of Dog Town Road (County Road 7), where a siding to the north begins. A timber storage yard and several tracks were located just west of a log pond. At Milepost 45.9 is the east end of the siding and where a track loops in to the old treatment plant. At one time, almost a half-dozen yard tracks were here, all located west of the private grade crossing at Milepost 46.5. Many company documents show Process City at Milepost 48 despite its actual location.

The name Process City came from the treatment processing that was performed here. Dierks built a small community north of the plant to house workers. You can see some of the old company houses by driving through the area.

To support the Process City facilities, a number of company houses were built by Dierks. Although the treatment plant is closed, some of these old houses still stand, like this one on Treating Plant Road.

While the plant is now gone, some of the tracks remain and see regular use. The turn to Valliant often leaves part of its train at Process City so that the tracks in De Queen are not overflowing. Later in the day, the Dierks Turn will come to here to pick up cars which head east to Union Pacific or various customers along the line.

The name of this street – Treating Plant Road – clearly tells the purpose of the Dierks plant that was built here in 1948. The plant was used to treat wood until Weyerhaeuser closed it in 2004.

48.1 LAST SPIKE SITE – The official last spike to connect the DeQueen & Eastern and the Texas, Oklahoma & Eastern was driven at 4:23pm on January 5, 1921, not far west of the KCS Crossing. This location was at the old Jefferson Highway crossing, an early road that connected Winnipeg, Manitoba, with New Orleans, Louisiana. This is near today's South Fourth Street.

As reported in several newspapers, both railroads were owned by the Dierks interests and it was fitting that the two routes "should have been united in the young and enterprising city where the first enterprise was born." Reportedly, the last spike wasn't driven by a Dierks family member, but by M. F. Allen, Second Vice President of both roads and superintendent of the DeQueen & Eastern. It should be noted that Matthew Fontaine Allen was involved with a number of Dierks family organizations such as several lumber companies and the Bank of Dierks. He was buried in Redmen Cemetery in De Queen upon his death in 1937.

Following the completion of the railroad, a large banquet was held that evening at De Queen, where a number of local officials spoke about how the railroad would benefit De Queen and open up large parts of Oklahoma and Arkansas to new farming development. Within a few days, the Chamber of Commerce assembled several committees to plan a celebration for when regular train service began.

In preparation for the opening of the line, the De-Queen & Eastern Railroad had filed a report with the Interstate Commerce Commission for permission to operate over the recently joined lines of the Texas, Oklahoma & Eastern and the DeQueen & Eastern. On April 23, 1921, the ICC determined that the request was outside the scope of their responsibility and that the two railroads were allowed to operate over the new line. With the ruling, the railroads announced that operations would begin on Saturday, May 14, 1921, with a large celebration. The day of celebration featured a parade, baseball games, and various performers. Both railroads operated special excursion trains to De Queen for the event, which had an estimated 8000 people attend, despite a light rain. The first train over the Texas, Oklahoma & Eastern arrived at the De Queen station, breaking through a rope of roses and other flowers held by a number of pretty girls. A full description of the event covered the front page of the Friday, May 20, 1921, issue of the *De Queen Bee*.

This eastbound approach signal for the DQ&E-KCS Diamond stands near where the last spike was driven on the Valliant to De Queen rail line.

48.3 **KCS CROSSING** – This automatic interlocking is a crossing with the Shreveport Subdivision of Kansas City Southern (KCS - Canadian Pacific Kansas City as of April 14, 2023). On the KCS, this is Milepost 433.8 and is known as D&E RRX, or the DeQueen & Eastern Railroad Crossing. While shown as an automatic interlocking, DeQueen & Eastern train crews receive permission to cross the diamond by pushing a button in a nearby control box. When permission is received, derails on each side of the crossing automatically are removed and a signal is given. This process is easily observed from Glasgow Road to the east of the diamond.

From the beginning, this was a busy railroad crossing. Several early reports stated that an "elaborate system of signals costing $15,000 was erected at the point at which the Texas, Oklahoma and Eastern crossed the Kansas City Southern line." The interlocking that was installed during January 1921 had 12 working mechanical levers and featured detector circuits and distant signals. In the railroad's August 3, 1947, employee timetable, it was stated that "KCS Crossing, De Queen, is interlocked and trains are governed by semaphores." This system lasted until Automatic Block Signals (ABS) were installed between Shreveport, Louisiana, and De Queen in 1951, and Centralized Traffic Control (CTC) signaling was installed northward to Heavener, Oklahoma, in 1954.

The signals at the DQ&E-KCS Diamond have changed over the years, and this old concrete signal foundation can still be found east of the diamond.

The DQ&E-KCS Diamond now uses a new OWLS-design frog. An OWLS (One-Way Low-Speed) frog is a unique type of frog where one line has no flangeway gap to cross, while the other line uses a slower flange-bearing design. At De Queen, the KCS line is the primary route and has no flange-way gap to cross, while the DeQueen & Eastern route uses the slower flange-bearing side of the frog, restricted to 10 miles per hour.

Eastbound TO&E D-12 is shown crossing the DQ&E-KCS Diamond in 2023 with a cut of freight cars for Dierks, Arkansas. The diamond is limited to 10mph for DeQueen & Eastern trains because of its design as a One-Way Low-Speed (OWLS) frog.

The KCS and De Queen

De Queen was one of the last towns along the KCS to receive rail service. On January 26, 1893, Arthur Edward Stilwell and his financial partners consolidated several railroads into the Kansas City, Pittsburg & Gulf Railroad Company (KCP&G), with a charter "to permit the extension of the line by construction, purchase, or lease to the Gulf of Mexico, through the states of Missouri, Kansas, Arkansas, Texas, and Louisiana."

A company also controlled by Stilwell, the Texas & Fort Smith (T&FS), was building track out of Texarkana, Arkansas. It reached Winthrop, Arkansas (39 miles from Texarkana), by December 1894, and the Little River (48 miles) by February 1895. By October 1895, the KCP&G had reached Poteau, Oklahoma, and the T&FS had reached Horatio, Arkansas (10 miles south of De Queen), leaving just a 120-mile gap. This gap was shortened when the KCP&G reached Mena, Arkansas, during August 1896. Within a few months, Stilwell announced that 1000 men were to be put to work on the construction of the railroad south of Mena, Arkansas, with an expected completion date in March 1897. By late December 1896, the track was completed to Cove, 35 miles north of De Queen. During February and March of 1897, contractors built the KCP&G line through De Queen, and the line was completed on March 10, 1897.

On October 30, 1897, all of the properties used to build the line were sold to the Kansas City, Pittsburg & Gulf Railroad Company. Soon the railroad was faced with large payments on various bonds and was unable to make them. Because of the default in the payment of interest on these bonds, the KCP&G was placed in the hands of receivers on April 1, 1899. The property was sold on March 22, 1900, to The Kansas City Southern Railway Company, which began operating the property on April 1, 1900.

As the railroad was improved and new operating patterns began, the KCS started to modify some of its divisions and crew change locations. By August 1909, the city of De Queen had raised more than $6000 as part of an effort to convince the railroad to move its shops and division headquarters to De

Queen. The following month, Kansas City Southern announced that it had awarded a contract to the Arnold Contracting Company of Chicago, Illinois, to build a new roundhouse and machine shop at De Queen. In October, the Ferguson Contracting Company was chosen to erect the new division terminal building. Section houses, a yard, and other facilities were also built. This made De Queen an important station on the railroad. A large KCS station was also built several blocks to the west of the DeQueen & Eastern depot, located between Stilwell and De Queen avenues. Today, only part of the KCS rail yard north of town remains.

In 1988, the north end of the large brick Kansas City Southern station at De Queen was still used by train crews and a few other employees, but the south end of the building was barely standing. The building was torn down within a few years.

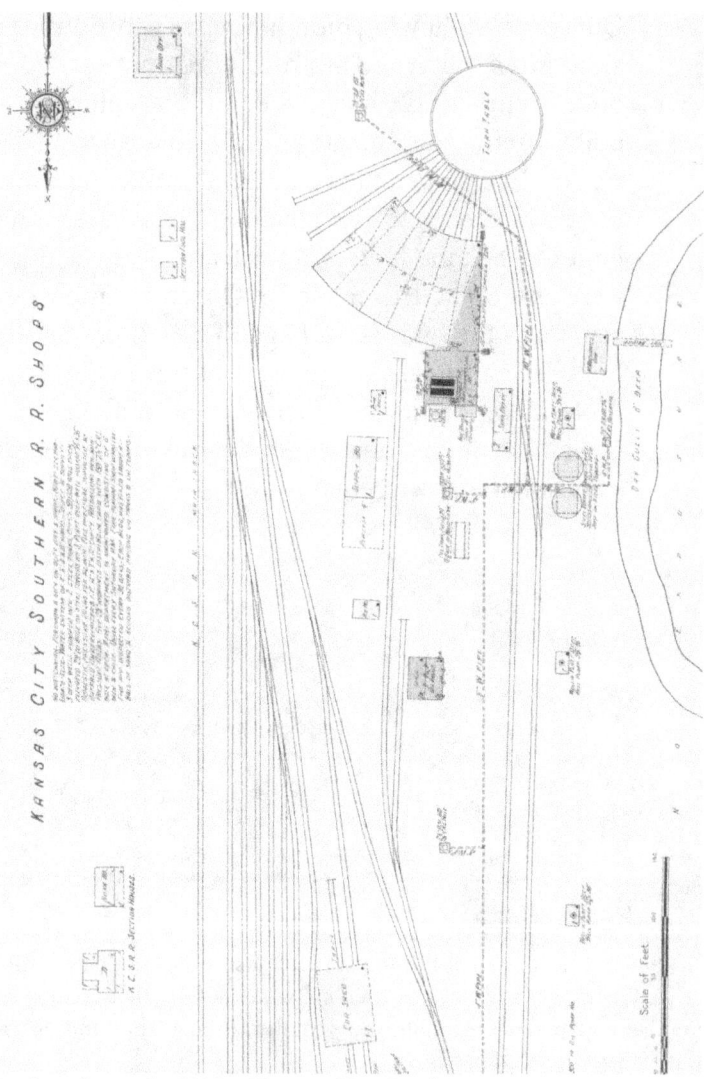

During the early 1900s, Kansas City Southern was reorganizing its train operations and establishing new shops and crew change points based upon the railroad's operations and new limits on crew operating hours. This led to a new KCS shops and roundhouse complex being built at De Queen, finished in 1910. These facilities were located on the west side of the KCS mainline, just north of today's DeQuincy Avenue. *Sanborn Fire Insurance Map from De Queen, Sevier County, Arkansas.* Sanborn Map Company, January 1914. Retrieved from the Library of Congress, https://www.loc.gov/item/sanborn00229_003/.

De Queen

De Queen is the administration headquarters of the DeQueen & Eastern and Texas, Oklahoma & Eastern railroads. It is also the county seat of Sevier County and its largest city.

Southwest Arkansas grew slowly, but was heavily influenced by commercial trade with Texas and Oklahoma. By the late 1800s, the area was still rural with the economy based upon farming, some timber production, and retail trade. The small community of Hurrah City developed in the area that is today called De Queen. By the early 1890s, it was clear that the Kansas City, Pittsburg & Gulf was going to build through the general area, but it wasn't until February and March of 1897 that the tracks were built through Sevier County.

The Arkansas Townsite Company acquired much of the area land and had surveyors create a plat and mark off blocks, streets, and alleys for a new town. Some sources state that the name Calamity was first used, but it soon became De Queen. The name De Queen was created by Arthur Stilwell to honor Jan de Goeijen, a Dutch coffee merchant who helped to sell $3 million of railroad stock. At the time, the Panic of 1893 had dried up funding for new railroad construction and Stilwell had used his European connections to keep money flowing. On April 26, 1897, sales of the various lots began and a town government was formed on June 3, 1897, with an official incorporation taking place on July 5, 1897. The town's population in the 1900 census was 1200. Much of the downtown burned on October 1, 1899, taking down at least fifty-four businesses. The wooden structures were quickly replaced by brick buildings due to a new brick factory and plans by the town to prevent future fires. Much of this downtown became the De Queen Commercial Historic District, added to the National Register of Historic Places in 2012.

As a part of the rebuilding of downtown De Queen, Dierks Lumber & Coal built a one-story brick building in 1900 at 314 De Queen Avenue, about three blocks west of the KCS depot. Soon located across the street from the Sevier County courthouse, the building featured "rounded arch parapets, recessed panels, ocular vents, transom windows, and cast-iron columns and threshold from the Twin City Foundry in Texarkana." Some sources state that The Big Store Commissary only lasted until 1908, but the firm was still advertising as a Dierks business in mid-1909. In fact, a one-page story about The Big Store can be found in the June 25, 1909, issue of the *De Queen Bee*. Eventually, the building was sold and began to house the Hayes Hardware store, which occupied the building until the 1980s. The building still stands and was listed on the National Register in December 1980.

The Dierks Big Store Commissary building still stands at 314 De Queen Avenue in De Queen, Arkansas.

Thanks to the railroad and all of the timber in the area, several sawmills soon opened at De Queen. These included the Williamson Brother's Lumber Company, Dierks Lumber & Coal, Forbes Lumber Company, Lambert Lumber Company, and W. H. Adams Lumber Company. All types of lumber and other wood products like barrel staves were shipped to market from these mills. Farm products like vegetables, peaches, and honey were also moved by the railroad.

The completion of the Dierk's railroads east to Dierks and west to Valliant during the early 1920s added to the rail network at De Queen, and provided an outlet to the St. Louis-San Francisco Railway. The operation of mills and logging camps in the area employed thousands, and Dierks operated a company store in downtown De Queen to serve them. More business moved to De Queen after a March 1905 vote that moved the county seat from Lockesburg to De Queen. Poultry also became a community staple after a large-scale hatchery opened in the 1920s. These industries led the population to grow to 2018 in 1910, 2517 in 1920, and 2938 in 1930.

Like most rural towns in the region, De Queen suffered through the Great Depression. A new post office was opened during this time that featured art as part of a government employment project. As the Dierks firm started moving out of the area, the company donated land to De Queen in 1954 that became the Herman Dierks Memorial Park. In 1969, Dierks sold its properties and organization to Weyerhaeuser, which soon had a smaller presence at De Queen.

This sign welcomes visitors to the Herman Dierks Memorial Park at De Queen, Arkansas. The land where the park sits was once where Dierks Lumber & Coal had their sawmill complex.

Next to the Herman Dierks Memorial Park are the grounds of the Sevier County Museum and its collections of local buildings and replicas. Among the collection is Texas, Oklahoma & Eastern caboose #84, donated by the railroad in 1992. At the same time, cabooses 81, 82 and 83 were sold to Klutts Equipment Company in Muskogee, Oklahoma, to use as offices.

The town suffered a small population loss during the 1940s and 1950s, but started growing again in the 1960s. The population hit 4633 in the 1990 census, at a time that the poultry industry became the dominant industry in town. Besides the economic boom, the poultry industry also changed the demographics of De Queen with a majority of the population now being Hispanic. In the 2020 census, De Queen had a population of 6105 people, 1865 households, and 1380 families residing in the city. Of this 3541 people were of a Hispanic background.

48.5 LITTLE BEAR CREEK BRIDGE – Heading east from the KCS diamond, the DeQueen & Eastern Railroad has their mainline pass around the south end of town. The railroad crosses Glasgow Road (Milepost 48.3), East Red Bridge Road (Milepost 48.4), and then the bridge over Little Bear Creek.

Eastbound trains on the DeQueen & Eastern cross the Little Bear Creek as they approach the West Wye Switch at De Queen.

Little Bear Creek forms about ten miles north of De Queen and flows southward. The stream created a wide valley used by the KCS mainline into De Queen. Little Bear Creek flows a short distance to the south and enters Bear Creek.

DQ&E D-29 shows its new Patriot Rail paint scheme as it pulls west across Little Bear Creek during March 2023.

48.5 WEST WYE SWITCH – This wye track is used to reach the railroad's locomotive shops, and the interchange tracks with Kansas City Southern (Canadian Pacific Kansas City). Because the original mileposts for the railroad included the route northward to the KCS, it is only 5600 feet between Milepost 48 and Milepost 51 on the mainline.

This wye was built as part of the Main Line Extension westward towards Broken Bow, Oklahoma. Railroad records dated November 22, 1920, report that the new wye track at De Queen was completed. Because the route northward is an important part of the DeQueen & Eastern, a description of this route is included here.

Late on a sunny March day in 2024, TO&E D-23 pulls a westbound train past the West Wye switch at De Queen.

48.6 NORTH WYE SWITCH – Immediately to the east are the shops of the DeQueen & Eastern Railroad. They include several modern steel shop buildings and office space. Just to their north is the brick machine shop, built in 1905 according to the National Register of Historic Places, as a part of the original shop construction. It is considered to be the only known period railroad shop building in the region.

Despite the 1905 date often quoted for the machine shop, the *Arkansas Gazette* had an article in their July 2, 1902, issue about new shops being built by the railroad. "A large addition to the De Queen and Eastern car shops has just been finished, and new machinery added, which about doubles the former capacity. New cars are constantly being turned out, and the road will soon have an equipment of rolling stock which will enable it to handle its growing freight traffic with the greatest facility."

A fire at 10pm on June 19, 1907, caused $40,000 in damage to the DeQueen & Eastern shops and also burned "locomotive No. 21". The railroad had new shops built by April 1908 that included a repair shed that measured 50x160 feet and a store house that measured 24x100 feet. The news also mentioned a new shop that measured 70x160 feet. These new facilities had been designed and built by C. B. Gimmill, the foreman for the company's pine sawmill. Some reports also state that there were plans for a six-bay locomotive roundhouse, but this structure was never built.

These early railroad shops had the ability to maintain and repair both the steam locomotives and freight cars used by the company. The equipment of other companies was also worked on. For example, a Little River Valley Railroad locomotive was reported as being repaired at the De Queen shops during October 1910. The complex included the machine shops and a 50'x160' engine house (often called the roundhouse). The DeQueen & Eastern Railroad Machine Shop is described as being "a tall and long single-story brick structure, with a monitor roof and modest Italianate styling." It was listed on the National Register of Historic Places on June 20, 1996. The report stated that the shop's "most distinctive features are the tall, arched window openings that light the walls on all four elevations and the monitor roof that runs along the top of the hipped roof. The interior largely retains its original work spaces and functional design." Work ceased at the DeQueen & Eastern Railroad Machine Shop shortly after World

War II as the railroad began to convert to diesel locomotives.

Besides the railroad's shops and depot facilities, the railroad also had an oil station and a water tank at De Queen in 1940. The steam locomotives of Dierks and its railroads initially burned wood, but later burned oil instead of coal or wood to reduce the danger of fire along the right-of-way, and to save money. The railroad's employee timetable in 1947 showed that the railroad had a 30-car siding, day telephone office, dispatcher, water, and an oil station at De Queen.

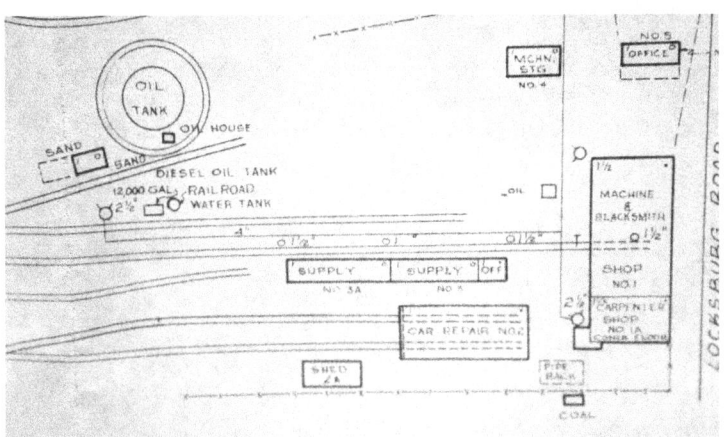

This map from 1948 shows the basic shop facilities that the railroad used at De Queen, Arkansas. Map, DeQueen & Eastern files, from author's collection.

Dieselization allowed other changes to be made at De Queen. In 1952, new diesel oil tanks were designed and installed. A new motor car building was built in 1959. This large building had barns for tractors and other equipment, plus four motorcar sheds. These four storage areas were for a telephone crew, a bridge gang, and several section crews. In 1990, a new locomotive sanding facility was installed at De Queen. Over the past several decades, even more changes have taken place as the depot location now features a large maintenance-of-way shop and improved offices are now found at the locomotive shops.

The December 25, 1920, issue of the *American Lumberman* included this photo of the DeQueen & Eastern shops at De Queen, Arkansas.

This is a view of the brick machine shop, built in 1905. It was a part of the original shop construction and is now listed on the National Register of Historic Places.

The modern DeQueen & Eastern shops and offices can be found south of the Stilwell Avenue grade crossing at De Queen, Arkansas.

South of the Stilwell Avenue grade crossing can also be found this new building which serves as a maintenance shop for the railroad.

For years, the railroad used this station building at De Queen, Arkansas. This view is from July 1988.

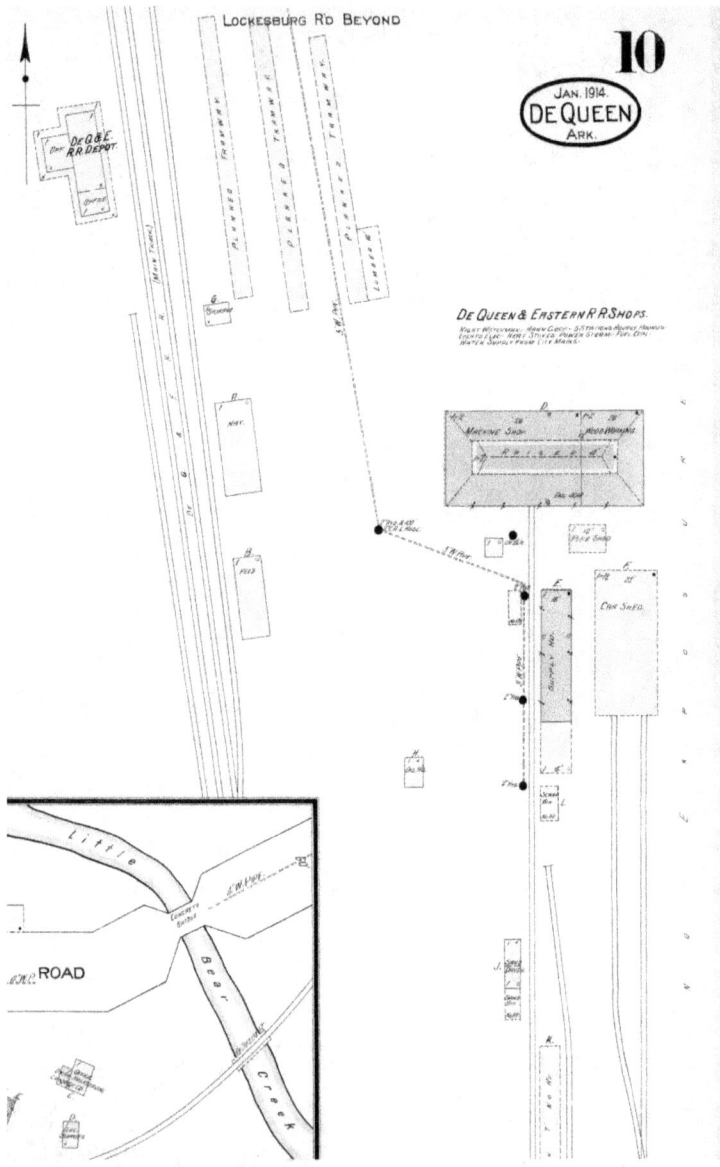

By 1908, the DeQueen & Eastern had built their shops just south of what became Stilwell Avenue. Among these buildings is the brick machine shop, which still stands today. *Sanborn Fire Insurance Map from De Queen, Sevier County, Arkansas.* Sanborn Map Company, January 1914. Map. Retrieved from the Library of Congress, https://www.loc.gov/item/sanborn00229_003/.

48.7 **STILWELL AVENUE** – Also known as Business U.S. 70, this road crossing once was known as Lockesburg Road. It has long been the primary route eastward out of town. The DeQueen & Eastern train station and office building was located west of their mainline and just south of the Stilwell Avenue grade crossing. A survey conducted in 1907-1908 reported that the elevation of the top of rail in front of the DeQueen & Eastern Railroad station was 370.1 feet.

The original De Queen station was the second depot built (October of 1902) on the entire DeQueen & Eastern. This De Queen depot was built of pine and measured 24' x 64'. It included a baggage room, two waiting rooms, and office space. The depot was an official telephone station for many years, and housed bulletin books and a train register. The standard clock for the entire railroad was maintained at De Queen. The KCS depot was to the west on Stilwell Avenue, described as being 100 yards from the DQ&E depot.

The station at De Queen was a topic covered in the ICC Tap Line Case hearing on December 17, 1910. The DeQueen & Eastern station was described as being a very large building "consisting of an agent's quarters, a general office for the accounting, waiting rooms, divided into white and colored divisions, freight and baggage room, and an express room, and all facilities needed by a railroad." The fact that it was not the office building of the Dierks Lumber & Coal Company was important in showing that the two companies were independent from each other. The station no longer stands. It was in bad shape by the late 1990s and was burned for practice by the De Queen fire department during February 1997.

Passenger service on the DQ&E/TO&E was never heavy, but it did operate during the early years. In July 1925, each morning except Sunday, train No. 2 would depart at 6:00am and head east to Dierks. It would return at 10:15am as train No. 1. Train No. 9, which operated daily except Sunday, was scheduled to depart De Queen for Valliant at 12:01pm. It would then return as No. 10 at 8:00pm. The Sunday-only No. 1 train would depart at 12:30pm, and return as No. 2 at 6:40pm.

In January 1945, the level of service was very similar. Mixed Train No. 9 left De Queen daily except Sunday at 6:35am and headed west to Valliant, arriving there at 10:30am. It turned as Mixed Train No. 10 at noon and arrived back at De Queen at 3:10pm. On Sundays, Train No. 1 used a motorcar, leaving De Queen at 8:45am and arriving at Valliant at 11:00am. It then left Valliant at 11:20am as Train No. 2, and arrived back at De Queen at 1:25pm. On the east end of the rail system, motorcar Train No. 6 departed De Queen at 1:00pm daily except Sunday. It then arrived at Dierks at 2:10pm, turned, and left at 3:40pm as Train No. 7. It finished its days at 4:45pm at De Queen.

The service remained this way for decades, and mail and passenger service on the DQ&E system ended in 1948.

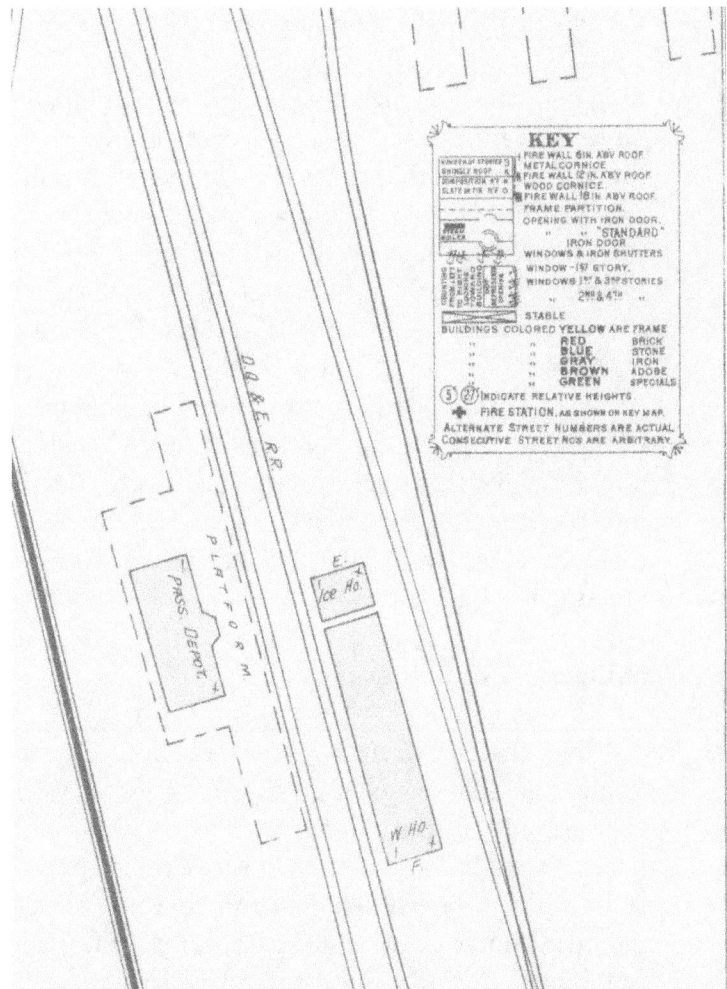

By 1904, the DeQueen & Eastern had built a passenger depot, located just south of where today's Stilwell Avenue crosses the tracks. A warehouse and ice house were across the tracks to the east. A hardwood lumber yard was further to the north on the line. Later, the warehouses were replaced by a lumber storage yard. *Sanborn Fire Insurance Map from De Queen, Sevier County, Arkansas.* Sanborn Map Company, September 1904. Map. Retrieved from the Library of Congress, https://www.loc.gov/item/sanborn00229_001/.

De Queen Wye and Interchange Track

When the De Queen & Eastern was originally built, the railroad was designed to bring timber to the mill and interchange loads of lumber with Kansas City Southern. A wye track once headed west, with the railroad's depot located between the wye's mainline switches. Both legs of the wye bridged over Little Bear Creek and joined together just east of the De Queen Ice, Light & Bottling Company facility. It then curved to the southwest, passing west of the Dyar-Armstrong Lumber Company's yellow pine sawmill. This track served as the KCS-DQ&E interchange track, which had a switch with the KCS mainline about where the Red Bridge Road grade crossing is today.

Shippers at Stilwell Avenue

When the DeQueen & Eastern was built, Dierks Lumber & Coal owned a great deal of property on the east side of town. This provided opportunities to lease or sell property to prospective rail shippers. Most of this property centered around Stilwell Avenue, also known as Lockesburg Road. By 1914, small warehouses for hay, lumber and other products were already standing. With the construction of the railroad towards Oklahoma, other businesses also leased property. One of the first to locate here was J. L. Cannon's potato house, a 10,000 bushel capacity potato drying house for sweet potatoes.

A series of bulk oil facilities were located here, with property leases signed in 1920 with the Magnolia Petroleum Company (Magnolia Oil Company) and Sinclair Oil Company. A similar lease was agreed upon in 1940 with the Arkansas Fuel Oil Company. The railroad even leased a track and some land to the Dierks Retail Lumber Yard for a sand pit in 1920.

48.8 INTERCHANGE TRACK SWITCH – Heading north, there is a small 3-track storage yard that can hold about 40 freight cars. It is also used as a transload facility for liquefied petroleum gas (LPG, or propane). Carloads of LPG are spotted here by the railroad and trucks then deliver to nearby customers, primarily poultry facilities.

A relatively new business at De Queen is the transload of propane from railcars to trucks for local delivery.

Where the yard is located, and the Herman Dierks Memorial Park to the east, was once the Williamson Brother's lumber mill. In early 1900, Dierks purchased the mill and established their Arkansas logging operations at De Queen. On May 5, 1909, the pine mill was destroyed by fire, but the hardwood mill and the planer mill were not damaged.

The mill complex was later replaced by a lumber mill at Dierks, Arkansas. During the logging days, the logging railroad had a 2-track locomotive shed east of the pine mill.

Heading to the northwest is the interchange track that heads to the Kansas City Southern rail yard.

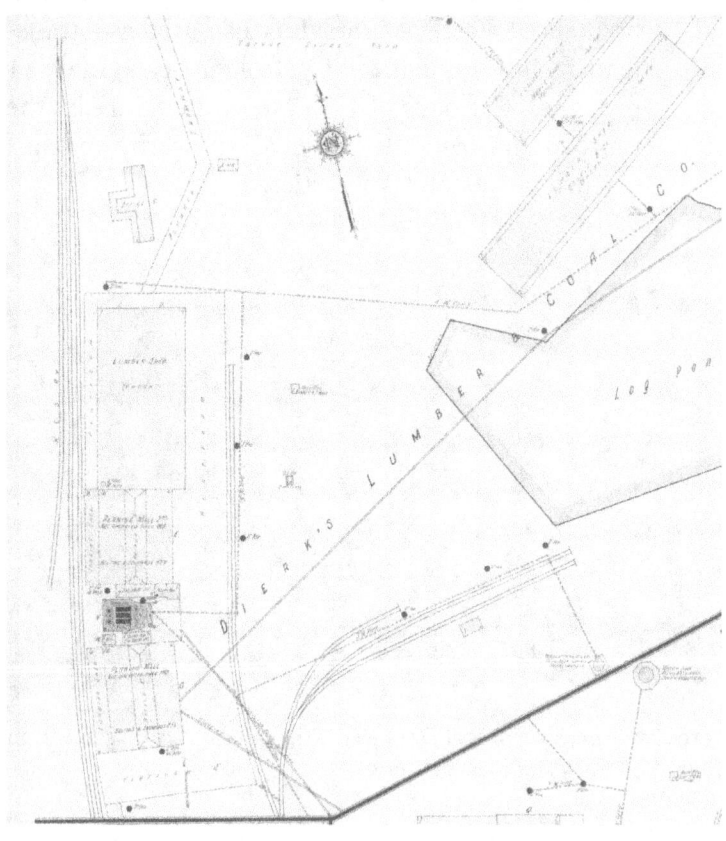

This Sanborn map from 1914 shows how the DeQueen & Eastern tracks separated the Dierks Lumber planing mill from the mainline of the Kansas City Southern. *Sanborn Fire Insurance Map from De Queen, Sevier County, Arkansas.* Sanborn Map Company, January 1914. Map. Retrieved from the Library of Congress, https://www.loc.gov/item/sanborn00229_003/.

In March 2023, TO&E D-12 is shoving a cut of interchange traffic into the Kansas City Southern yard at De Queen, Arkansas.

49.1 CONTROL POINT D&E CONNECTION – This is the junction between the KCS and DeQueen & Eastern. The DQ&E interchanges with the KCS by entering their mainline and then crossing to the west to enter the KCS freight yard. KCS employee timetables list Control Point D&E Connection as being at their Milepost 432.9. They also state that "KCS Yard Track No. 1 is designated as D&E Delivered Interchange Track (D&E to KCS) and Yard Track No. 2 is designated as D&E Received Interchange Track (KCS to D&E)."

TO&E locomotive D-12 is shown pulling an interchange train out of the Kansas City Southern past Control Point D&E Connection.

48.8 EAST WYE SWITCH – DeQueen & Eastern employee timetables often showed this area to be Shopton, named for the railroad's shops that are located just north of here. This switch is located immediately west of the Arkansas Highway 41 (Lakeside Drive) overpass. Highway 41 begins at U.S. Highway 70B in De Queen and heads south to Texas State Highway 8 at the Texas state line. A short siding exists on the south side of the mainline, and it is often used to hold cars for the Dierks and Valliant Turns.

This construction marker can be found on the Arkansas Highway 41 bridge over the DeQueen & Eastern tracks near the East Wye Switch.

Arkansas Highway 41 bridge over the DeQueen & Eastern can be a great vantage point to watch trains switch at De Queen. Here, TO&E D-12 leads two more locomotives as they put together the Turn for Dierks.

The first few miles of track to the east were not built by Dierks or the DeQueen & Eastern Railroad. When the Dierks Lumber & Coal Company bought the Williamson lumber mill for $250,000 in 1900, the deal included a number of facilities. This included the sawmill, dry kilns, a planing mill, and a partly-completed five-mile logging railroad that was being built east as far as the Cossatot River.

The mileposts through this area can be a bit confusing. The mileposts actually head north around the wye to the KCS interchange and then back to here before heading on to the east. For the mainline, this means that there are no Mileposts 49 or 50. Instead, the distance between Milepost 48 and Milepost 51 is 5600 feet, or about 1.06 miles.

51.1 BEAR CREEK BRIDGE – There are actually two small timber pile trestles that are used to cross Bear Creek. The western bridge is 10 spans long while the eastern bridge is six spans long.

Bear Creek forms in the mountains a dozen miles northeast of De Queen. It flows south from De Queen and into the Little River west of Horatio, about ten miles from here. Bear Creek is a very common name in Arkansas, and the state even once had the unofficial nickname of The Bear State.

51.1 WEST SWITCH THREE-TRACK YARD – This yard is almost a mile long and includes a center through track and tracks to the north and south, used to build trains and swap blocks between various trains.

52.0 EAST SWITCH THREE-TRACK YARD – This switch is located a short distance west of Arkansas

Highway 329 (Milepost 52.3). This highway is only eight miles long and connects De Queen with Lockesburg. The elevation here is 377 feet.

At the Highway 329 grade crossing is a Pilgrim's Pride hatchery complex.

On a sunny March day, the Dierks Turn, pulled by TO&E D-12, passes the Pilgrim's Pride hatchery complex east of De Queen, Arkansas.

54.0 EAST END DE QUEEN YARD LIMITS – Located at the grade crossing with Sevier County Road 102 is the east end of the De Queen yard limits. The track heading east to Milepost 74.6 is operated using Track Warrant Control.

DeQueen & Eastern locomotive D-29 is shown heading west, entering the De Queen yard limits at the Sevier County Road 102 grade crossing.

56.2 GENEVA – This station was located near the grade crossing with Sevier County Road 15 at an elevation of 360 feet. To the east of the grade crossing is a private grade crossing near the Geneva Missionary Baptist Church at Milepost 56.6. Old railroad grades can be seen in the area.

This sign is about all that still carries the name of the former station of Geneva, Arkansas.

The *Arkansas Gazette* (December 3, 1901) reported that the DeQueen & Eastern had reached this general area by late 1901. The article noted that the railroad had been completed to "a point near Jones Nally's, a mile or two west of the Cossatot river." The Nalley family owned land in the area and has a long history associated with the Lockesburg area.

Before the lumber company and railroad opened permanent facilities along the line, a moving store served the loggers and railroaders. The *De Queen Bee* of June 27, 1902, reported on the operation. "The Dierks Lumber and Coal Company has a store on wheels, in charge of Paul K. Marsh. It is a handsomely painted car, stocked with all kinds of merchandise, and travels where its manager wishes it to cover the DQ&E."

Geneva was never much more than a side track and small community. Reportedly, this was one of the first log loading stations on the line; however, it was seldom more than a flag stop for the railroad. The Williamson lumber company used this as a timber loading point and it took the name Logville. By the late 1890s, the community was known as Hortense, a French feminine given name that comes from Latin meaning gardener. At this time, there were two schools in the community. In 1906, the community was renamed Geneva, and it grew by the end of the decade to include a post office, two cotton gins, two stores, two sawmills, two grist mills, and a telephone exchange. In 1910, the *American Lumberman* magazine reported that there were three stores, a church, a school, and a sawmill at Geneva. The post office closed in 1911, and as the timber was cut, the community lost its importance. In 1921, the C. B. Smith lumber mill was still active at Geneva. By the 1930s, only a single store remained open. Today, the site is marked by several houses and the Geneva Missionary Baptist Church.

Geneva was a regular or flag passenger stop for many years, but the station was never very fancy. Initially, the railroad's office was located in the general store of A. L. Middleton, who was hired as the local agent. In 1910, the hearing for the ICC Tap Line Case reported that the Geneva station was "what is called a house car with three rooms which accommodate the agents and also the white and colored passengers." The term house car apparently meant that the depot was constructed using a retired freight car. In 1925, passenger train No. 2 stopped here at 6:15am daily except Sunday. It would turn at Dierks and pass by heading westward as train No. 1 at 9:48am. In 1947, Geneva was down to simply a 5-car siding.

57.8 COSSATOT SET OUT – There was once a spur track to the north on the west side of the Cossatot River. It served a series of gravel pits in the area, plus some timber loading. A vague report about a community and railroad station near here was made in the January 23, 1902, *Arkansas Gazette*. The report stated that Hovensville, "the second station out on the De Queen and Eastern is largely a town of tents, but it is only about a month old and will improve with age." Little else was ever documented about the community.

During the first few decades of the twentieth century, there was a "Cossatot Park" here. The Cossatot Park Association was chartered in 1907 with John Tobin as president. Tobin owned and operated the John L. Tobin Hardware Store in De Queen, a firm which sold hardware, furniture, and dry goods. The park was very popular on hot summer days due to the cool waters of the Cossatot River. An early article in the *De Queen Bee* newspaper reported that "Cossatot Park is a popular resort eight miles east of De Queen at the point where the DeQueen & Eastern railroad crosses the Cossatot river. There are good facilities for bathing, boating, fishing and picnicking at this place. The DeQueen & Eastern railroad runs special trains to the park when occasion demands. The park management has some good river bottom land at this place and has under consideration a plan to convert part of it into an experimental and demonstration farm to show what can be done with Sevier county soil."

In 1916, the park's bath house was rebuilt into a hotel to house the workers involved with rebuilding the railroad's bridge over the river. By this time, the park had pretty much been replaced with the Reunion Grounds, a park on the Cossatot River where the De Queen-Lockesburg Highway bridged across the waterway.

This area served a new purpose during 1921 as gravel was obtained here to ballast the new Main Line Extension between De Queen and the Mountain Fork River. By Fall 1921, more than 300 carloads of gravel had been hauled from here and spread along the new rail line.

SUNDAY
Summer Excursions
TO
COSSATOT PARK
Via DE QUEEN & EASTERN R. R.

Train Will Be Run as Follows:

East Bound			West Bound	
Lv 9:30 a.m.	Lv 2:03 p m	**De Queen**	Ar 1:00 p m	Ar 6:30 p m
Lv 10 a. m	Ar 2:30 p m / Lv 4:15 p m	**Cossatot Park**	Ar 1:55 p m	Ar 6:10 p m
Lv 10:15 a m	Lv 4:30 p m	**Lockesburg**	Ar 1 p m	Ar 6 p m
Lv 10:55 a m	Lv 4:50 p m	**Provo**	Ar 12:35 p m	Ar 5:40
Ar 11 a m	Ar 5:10 p m	**Dierks**	Lv 12:15 p m / Lv 5:20 p m	

These trains will run Sundays during the months of June, July and August.

Boating, bathing, good fishing and other amusements.

The DeQueen & Eastern operated special trains to Cossatot Park for several years, as shown in this advertisement in the July 3, 1908, issue of the *De Queen Bee* newspaper.

Excursion Train

The De Queen & Eastern will run a special train to Cossatot Park every Thursday afternoon till further notice. Round trip rate of 30 cents will be charged. Train will leave De Queen at 3:30 p. m., leave the park for Lockesburg at 5:30, leave the park for De Queen at 6 p. m.

C. C. RAY,

G. P. A.

In 1909, the DeQueen & Eastern operated regular trips to Cossatot Park on Thursdays from De Queen and Lockesburg. This announcement in the *De Queen Bee* newspaper provides the details.

58.0   COSSATOT RIVER – The railroad crosses this nationally famous white water river using a Pratt through truss with a series of deck plate girder spans off each end. There is a long timber pile trestle at the east end of the structure. Reports state that the original piers have been replaced with newer cement piers.

Construction of the Cossatot River bridge was news that was reported in the *De Queen Bee* (February 14, 1902) and *Arkansas Gazette* (February 20, 1902). Both issues stated:

De Queen – Steel for the De Queen and Eastern's bridge across the Cossatot arrived Sunday. The roadbed is completed to and beyond the river. Ties are being placed this week, and in a few days the iron horse will be able to see its reflection in the clear water of the classic Cossatot. In the meantime Lockesburg is alive with expectancy and with patience and buoyant hope, awaiting the shriek of the locomotive.

Another article on April 23, 1902, reported that the bridge had been completed and that trains would "be running into Lockesburg by the middle of May." Han Dierks, who at the time was president of the Dierks Lumber and Coal Company, visited the bridge site upon its completion. He also visited Lockesburg as part of the inspection trip. One of the major issues in April was choosing a location for the Lockesburg depot.

During Fall 1916, a new bridge was installed over the Cossatot River. Built by the Rogers Construction Company, the new bridge was required to handle the heavier traffic that had developed on the railroad. As stated at the time, "the new bridge is to be of massive type and of great strength." Despite this, a portion of the steel bridge was washed out during flooding in May 1920, when many parts of the railroad were under water between Valliant and Dierks.

The Cossatot River is 90 miles long and is a principal tributary of the Little River. The river begins in the Ouachita Mountains southeast of Mena, Arkansas, and flows to the south through the Ouachita National Forest. The term Cossatot is an Americanized version of an Indian term meaning skull crusher, an appropriate name for this river that features stretches of Class II to V whitewater. It has been called "the most challenging section of whitewater between the Smokies and the Rockies." The water in this area is probably the most gentle along its entire route. The Cossatot is listed as a National Wild and Scenic River and an Arkansas Natural and Scenic River.

61.7 LOCKESBURG – Lockesburg could have been De Queen, but when the surveyors working for the Kansas City, Pittsburg & Gulf passed through the region, the residents apparently were not very cooperative about assisting in the railroad's construction. While other communities offered free land and even showed a willingness to buy railroad bonds, Lockesburg's exorbitant demands for right-of-way costs forced the railroad to seek another route. Instead, the community had to wait until the DeQueen & Eastern extended their line to here from De Queen and started passenger service for the twelve-mile stretch between De Queen and Lockesburg on June 14, 1902.

This highway sign marks the city limits of Lockesburg, once a busy station on the DeQueen & Eastern.

Lockesburg, spelled Lockesburgh by the post office until 1893, came about because the southern portion of Sevier County was used to create Little River County in 1867. This left the old county seat of Paraclifta in the extreme southeast corner of the county. A commission was created in 1869 to locate a new county seat in the center of the county, and the property of the Locke brothers (Matthew, James, and W. T.) was chosen, especially after they agreed to sell 120 acres to the county for $10. The new community was immediately surveyed and platted, and then named for the Locke brothers. Lots were soon sold and $25,000 was spent on a new two-story brick courthouse in 1871. A new jail was added in 1888 for an additional $1000.

Even before the county government buildings were erected, the Lockesburgh post office opened on May 3, 1870, with Matthew W. Locke serving as the first postmaster. Several businesses soon opened and churches followed – Methodist Episcopal in 1872 and Cumberland Presbyterian in 1878. With all of the activity, Lockesburg was incorporated on September 27, 1878, and its population was 256 in the 1880 census.

By the 1890 census, the population was 451 and Lockesburg had six general stores, one grocer, one drug store, four physicians, five practicing attorneys, four blacksmiths, two newspapers, and one hotel. In 1893, the post office dropped the 'h' and became Lockesburg. Why the change? In 1890, the United States Board of Geographic Names was created to bring consistency to the spellings of various locations. One of its first actions was to declare that all towns ending in 'burgh' must drop the 'h' in the spirit of uniformity.

The year 1893 also saw the establishment of the Hesperian High School, the first high school in Sevier County, located on property donated by Matthew W. Locke. It was renamed Lockesburg High School in 1924. Even though Lockesburg was the county seat, it was still a small town based upon local farming. But it was a pretty town in 1897, according to the *Missouri and Arkansas Farm Newspaper*, which stated the following.

> *We enter Lockesburg, a small village of 400 people, with many pretty homes. Modern frame houses, large yards shaded with massive, forest trees, and tastefully kept green lawns and flowers, shrubs and fruits. The town comprising (sic) a brick court house in the center of a square, which is lavishly shaded with large forest trees, around which is the business part of the town, comprising fifteen or twenty stores of various kinds.*

The next major change in Lockesburg was the arrival of the DeQueen & Eastern Railroad during late May 1902, which allowed other industries to develop. The Bank of Lockesburg incorporated later that year on October 14th. A negative step took place in 1905 when the county seat moved to De Queen. Over the next two decades, the downtown area remained the home of several dozen businesses, and a series of companies that relied upon the railroad came and went. These included the Rummuel Brothers hardwood mill (1907), which later became Dickes & Rummel Brothers, a firm that established "a box factory in connection with their lumber plant, to manufacture crates and boxes for fruit shippers." There were also the Lockesburg Brick Company (1912); Shannon & Johnson feed business (1921); the Lockesburg Lumber Company through purchase of the Federal Lumber Company in 1921; and the Acme Lumber Company (1923), which was acquired by the Lockesburg Lumber Company in 1925. Additionally, several packing houses handled local farm products.

A June 1909 report stated that Lockesburg featured a railroad station, cotton platform, a siding, a passing track, and cattle pens with a loading chute. The Farmers' Union had a cotton warehouse and two seed warehouses. From Lockesburg, the railroad reportedly shipped cotton seed, cotton, cattle, hogs, sheep, lumber, crossties, peaches, potatoes, and radishes. As shown, farming and ranching were important to Lockesburg, and were for decades the primary businesses conducted there. For example, the DeQueen & Eastern handled a shipment of six carloads of cattle from Lockesburg to Kansas City in December 1909. An article published in the January 1914 issue of *KCS Current Events – An Industrial and Agricultural Magazine,* provided information about the businesses at Lockesburg that shipped by rail. For those not familiar with the term, truck means assorted vegetables like spinach, greens, beans and peas, etc.

A large business is done in the shipping of livestock and hardwood timbers in the form of railroad ties, barrel staves, fence posts, mine timbers, and lumber. The cotton shipments run from 3,000 to 5,000 bales per year. A fine fruit and truck growing industry has grown up

within the last three or four years, and peaches,
potatoes, truck, etc., are shipped in carload lots.

A report from 1920 stated that the population was 794 and that the town had the usual collection of stores and businesses, plus a weekly newspaper, a bank, a flour mill and a brick factory. The 1921 *Arkansas Marketing and Industrial Guide* provided a list of industries at Lockesburg, which included the Lockesburg Brick Company, Lockesburg Gin Company (cotton), W. T. Abbott grist mill, Fear Brothers (lumber mill), Federal Lumber Company, R. B. Friday & Son (lumber mill), T. W. Parks (sweet potato curing house), Lockesburg Warehouse Company, and Farmers Union Warehouse Company. Soon, the Duncan Lumber Company of Kansas City established a planer and sawmill west of Lockesburg.

The population held steady until the 1950s when it dropped to 511 in 1960, caused by losses in the timber industry. Despite the population growing again, reaching 739 residents in 2010, the Lockesburg School District consolidated into the De Queen District in 2006. This may have been a sign of the future as the population dropped back to 594 in the 2020 census. There are still several dozen businesses at Lockesburg, including banks, pharmacies, a gas station, restaurants, and others that are generally found in rural Arkansas communities. Tourism, thanks to the nearby Cossatot River State Park-Natural Area and the Pond Creek National Wildlife Refuge Area, also helps to keep the town hopping.

The Cantaloupe Crisis

During the late 1910s, T. W. Park and others organized at Lockesburg for the purpose of growing and shipping cantaloupes and peaches. Supporting the efforts was C. C. Ray, manager of the freight department of the DeQueen & Eastern, who stated that the railroad would build a shed and take care of their shipments. The farmers soon were growing large volumes of the crops and contracted with the railroad for the needed freight cars. However, not enough cars were delivered and some of the crop rotted before it could be shipped. This resulted in a lawsuit against the railroad that went all the way to the Supreme Court of Arkansas in late 1920.

As reported in the hearing, T. W. Park "ordered 100 cars for cantaloupes and 12 cars for peaches from the depot agent. The depot agent notified the manager, and the manager made an arrangement with the American Refrigerator Transit Company to furnish iced cars to be used in the shipment of the cantaloupes and peaches. The DeQueen & Eastern Railroad Company was only 27 miles long, and Lockesburg was the only station on its line where cantaloupes and peaches were shipped. It connected with the Kansas City Southern Railway Company, and could only make a contract with the American Refrigerator Transit Company for refrigerator cars, because that company was the only one operating on the line of the Kansas City Southern Railway Company. The defendant railway company furnished Park and others 92 cars for cantaloupes, and 10 cars for peaches. The custom was that Park would notify the agent of the railway company at Lockesburg how many cars he would need for the next shipment. On a certain day he ordered cars for the next shipment, and the cantaloupes were placed in the shed at the depot prepared for that purpose. The railway company failed to furnish the refrigerator cars because the refrigerator company failed to deliver them to it." The Arkansas Supreme Court supported the decision that the DeQueen & Eastern was liable for the loss of the cantaloupes due to the failure to deliver the iced refrigerator cars that had been ordered.

The DeQueen & Eastern Railroad at Lockesburg

After having lost the Kansas City Southern, the citizens of Lockesburg decided to support the construction of the DeQueen & Eastern Railroad. During November 1901, the citizens raised money to give the railroad a $15,000 bonus if the railroad came through the town. In return, the railroad proposed a donation of $20,000 in cash and right-of-way. To qualify for the payment, the railroad had to be completed and operating to Lockesburg within eight months. The first passenger train arrived on June 14, 1902, and the railroad's first depot was built here and opened during September. An early description of the depot was that it had a first floor for passenger and freight services, and an upper level with general offices for the DeQueen & Eastern and Dierks Lumber officials.

Lockesburg was a significant part of the testimony at the Interstate Commerce Commission Tap Line Case hearing of December 17, 1910. The reason was that Lockesburg was viewed by the ICC as being out of the way of the railroad as it built eastward to Dierks. When asked, the management of the DeQueen & Eastern stated that "it was about six miles that we went out of our way, that is, went out of the way of the Dierks Lumber & Coal Company's timber, to reach Lockesburg." It was added that it was a very expensive railroad to build as there were two very deep cuts near Lockesburg that were "about 25 feet deep and the two of them combined are two or three hundred yards long." It was noted that while the citizens of Lockesburg donated $15,000 to the railroad, the route via Lockesburg, as opposed to going in a straight line, cost the company between $75,000 and $100,000 additional.

The hearing also looked at the facilities at Lockesburg. This included a five-room section house and "a complete station which has the agent's quarters and white and black waiting room and freight and express quarters."

While Lockesburg was established before the railroad arrived, and Dierks Lumber & Coal Company never had a major presence in the town, there were still a number of tracks and rail facilities here. A map from 1913 shows that there was a siding on the north side of the mainline. Along this siding were shippers like the Farmers' Union cotton warehouse, and the cotton seed storage warehouse of United Oil Mills and Arkansas Cotton Oil. At this time, the depot was south of the tracks and described as being 1/4 mile northeast of the old courthouse.

In 1925, the depot was an official telephone station, handing out train orders and instructions to train crews, selling passenger train tickets, and handling the billing of freight shipped from Lockesburg. The town was also a regular passenger stop for many years. In 1925, passenger train No. 2 stopped here at 6:45am daily except Sunday. It would turn at Dierks and be here as train No. 1 at 9:35am.

Little remains of the railroad facilities that stood in Lockesburg in 1913. This Sanborn map shows the general area around the DeQueen & Eastern depot. *Sanborn Fire Insurance Map from Lockesburg, Sevier County, Arkansas.* Sanborn Map Company, August 1913. Map. Retrieved from the Library of Congress, https://www.loc.gov/item/sanborn00286_001/.

In 1945, the railroad expanded its track facilities at Lockesburg to allow Dierks Lumber & Coal to load logs here. A railroad report stated that the House Track was extended 429 feet, and 1222 feet of the old Long Passing Track were relayed at a cost of $3,239.52. The costs were billed to the lumber company. In 1947, the DeQueen & Eastern called Lockesburg a day telephone office and reported that there was a 12-car siding.

The DeQueen & Eastern still has a siding at Lockesburg, plus this station sign located near the west switch.

The Dierks Turn is shown heading east past the siding at Lockesburg in 2023.

Even as the number of local rail customers declined, the siding at Lockesburg remained. In 1979, the railroad timetable showed that it had a capacity of 40 freight cars. In 1985, it was shown to hold 70 cars in its 4138-foot length. While the old siding was shown to be northeast of the old courthouse by Sanborn, a map from 1951 shows several sidings to the northwest of Lockesburg. Today, a long siding is still located south of the mainline in this area, with Park Avenue crossing the tracks at Milepost 61.7. The west switch is located just east of the Milepost 61 sign alongside Hilltop Lane. Not far east of the siding, the railroad passes under U.S. Highway 59/71/371, known as North Camellia locally, at Milepost 62.0. This bridge was built in 1938 at a cost of $28,109.60 as part of a nationwide grade crossing elimination project.

DQ&E D-29 is shown passing under the Milepost 62 highway bridge at Lockesburg as it heads west towards De Queen, Arkansas. Notice the top of the hill that is located under the bridge, creating downhill grades in both directions from Lockesburg.

Not far east of Lockesburg, the railroad curves to the north, following the route of Bellville Creek, which it crosses several times using short timber pile trestle bridges. The tracks head generally north to Provo, where they turn to the northeast. Along this route, the railroad first drops from an elevation of 405 feet at Lockesburg (406.6 feet at the top of rail in front of the station) to 380 feet at Bellville Creek. Then it climbs up the waterway's valley, peaking at an elevation of about 440 feet before dropping down to Provo at an elevation of 394 feet (390.2 feet on top of rail in front of the station). Almost this entire route is through thick pine forests, planted for future harvesting.

The Azalea Street Bridge

The remains of a second highway overpass can be found a block east of the U.S. Highway 71 bridge at Lockesburg. This bridge, located on North Azalea Street, stood until the afternoon of June 15, 2005, when the last six cars of a westbound 75-car train derailed and knocked part of the structure down. According to local sources, the bridge was built in 1902 and was considered to be historically significant. Despite efforts to plan for a new bridge, and a payment of $350,000 by the railroad, no bridge was ever built.

64.5 **COULTER SPUR** – Coulter Spur was listed as a flag stop between Lockesburg and Provo by 1913, but was not listed in 1916. It was located on the Coulter family farm alongside Bellville Creek. Coulter Spur is now located in the center of a large pine plantation, near property still known as the Coulter Farm, reached via Coulter Lane. During the early 1920s, a number of wells were drilled in the area looking for oil and natural gas. In 1923, Kansas City Southern reported on this activity and stated that work on the Coulter well, east of Lockesburg, was progressing.

Coulter is an old name in Sevier County. James Madison Coulter arrived in the area with his parents in 1836 and began construction of his home in 1861. Soon, however, he fled to Texas to avoid the Civil War. He returned to Arkansas after the war and was elected as county judge for Sevier County, and served for a year. Other members of the family settled throughout the region. A short distance north of Lockesburg is the Coulter Memorial Garden, located just south of the Lockesburg Cemetery and the Odd Fellows Cemetery.

68.8 PROVO – The first community in this area was Farribaville, located about a mile north of today's Provo. One of the first settlers was W. M. Wilson, who arrived there in 1857. A post office opened at Farribaville in 1868, but it closed and moved to Provo in 1903 when the railroad was being built to here.

The new community was to be named Saline, but because there was already a Saline post office in Arkansas, the railroad chose the name of Provo for the new town to be located near the Saline River. The Provo depot opened in April of 1903, and it was the third depot built by the railroad. Several reports state that Provo was named and created by Dierks officials, essentially being a company town while the area timber was cut. Early reports about the new community stated that "the Dierks Lumber & Coal company was to build a store, hotel and warehouse" here.

In 1908, W. A. Gelbach led a survey team along the railroad as part of a leveling and mapping project. In 1912, an adjustment of precise leveling survey checked the initial measurements. It reported that the elevation of the top of rail in front of the Provo station was 390.2 feet.

In 1914, E. G. Mattingly and J. A. Mattingly came to Provo from Kentucky and helped to establish the Cumberland Presbyterian Church, renamed Provo Cumberland Presbyterian Church in 1916. A white frame building was erected in 1921, using materials donated by the Dierks Lumber & Coal Company and moved by the DeQueen & Eastern Railroad. The church still stands. Edmund Grant Mattingly lived here the remainder of his life and is buried in the nearby McHorse Cemetery, located at the Pleasant Hill Missionary Baptist Church.

The former lumber and railroad community of Provo can be reached using Provo Road northeast of Lockesburg, Arkansas.

By 1910, the railroad had built a five-room section house at Provo, described as being "painted and in good condition." A lumber company was here for a short time, and in 1922, an Arkansas report listed Provo as an "important village" in Sevier County. Why wasn't stated. However, nearby Dierks and Lockesburg kept Provo pretty small with only a few stores and several hundred residents. Despite the size of Provo, it was a regular stop for the mixed trains, and it was the home of a company telephone station. In 1925, passenger train No. 2 stopped here at 7:05am daily except Sunday. It would turn at Dierks and be here as train No. 1 at 9:05am.

Immediately after World War II, there was a 6-car siding at Provo. The depot was shown to be a day telephone office. In 1954, the Provo post office closed, and the community is now a scattered grouping of houses. The railroad still had a 1126-foot-long (17 freight cars) siding at the south edge of the former townsite in 1985. Today, only the south end of the siding still exists.

This view shows the remains of the siding, the mainline, and a pile of new crossties for track work at Provo, Arkansas.

The same pile of new ties is being passed by the Dierks Turn during March 2023.

70.5 SALINE RIVER BRIDGE – During 1907-1908, a survey was conducted along the DeQueen & Eastern Railroad. It established a painted square bench mark on the southeast pier of the bridge over the Saline River, identified as being at an elevation of 353.15 feet. This bridge features a Pratt through truss span over the main channel of the river, and then a series of I-beam spans off each end, set on timber piles. A short distance to the northeast is a long timber pile trestle that allows water to move through the railroad grade during times of high water. The bridge was completed during late January 1906, and it still sits on its original steel cylinder piers, unique for the region. Currently, trains are restricted to 10 miles per hour across the Saline River Bridge.

DeQueen & Eastern D-29 is shown heading west across the Saline River Bridge and past Milepost 70. This bridge is an original through truss structure and has a 10mph speed limit.

There are actually two rivers that use the Saline name in Arkansas. One forms in the central part of the Ouachita Mountains and flows into the Ouachita River in south Arkansas. The Saline River that this bridge crosses also forms in the Ouachita Mountains, but this time in the southern part of the hills, in a part of the Ouachita National Forest in Polk County. This Saline River flows 80 miles to the south, eventually entering Millwood Lake, a part of the Little River. For much of its length, the river forms the border between Sevier and Howard counties in southwestern Arkansas.

The railroad continues to the northeast to reach the sawmill town of Dierks. The railroad is lined by trees just about the entire route.

County Line

To the west of the Saline River is Sevier County, while to the east is Howard County. **Sevier County** is located in southwest Arkansas and borders the state of Oklahoma. The Little River forms the southern boundary of the county, while the Saline River borders the east side. Settlement began about 1810, and when the Choctaw started moving out of Mississippi in 1820, the tribe received land in southwest Arkansas. In 1825, they agreed to move to Indian Territory, but some stayed or worked in the area.

Sevier County was created on October 17, 1828, named for Ambrose Sevier, U.S. Senator from Arkansas. The county has since then been cut up to create other counties. The first county seat was Paraclifta, but was moved to Lockesburg in 1871 after the Lockes family donated land for the community. It finally moved to De Queen in 1905. The county's economy has historically been based upon agriculture – corn, cotton, strawberries, cucumbers, sweet potatoes, watermelons, and cantaloupes. Timber has also been important. Seventy percent of the county is still timberland, and the current population is about 17,000 residents.

Howard County was formed on April 17, 1873, from parts of Hempstead, Sevier, Polk and Pike Counties. It was named after state Senator James H. Howard. The first county seat was Center Point, but it moved to Nashville in 1905 after much of Center Point burned. Howard County has always had a farming economy, with cotton the most important crop. Because of the large number of workers required to plant and pick cotton, the population of Howard County peaked in 1920 with 18,565 residents. However, the fields played out and the industry moved elsewhere, with the last bale of cotton ginned in the fall of 1971. Sheep and wool were another major product produced in the county, but that ended by 1930. Peaches were grown here in large volumes until the 1950s. Today, poultry, timber, light manufacturing, and tourism drive much of the economy, and the population was 12,785 in the 2020 census.

70.8 **BRIDGE** – This 160-foot-long timber pile trestle can be found where the tracks curve more to the north. The stream that flows under the trestle comes off the low hills to the east. It then flows into Holly Creek, which flows into the Saline River a quarter-mile downstream. The railroad follows Holly Creek all the way to Dierks.

While the railroad generally stays in the woods as it heads north to Dierks, poultry is strong in this area. There are a number of large poultry farms to the east, thanks to firms like Tyson, which has a large feed mill and processing plant at nearby Nashville, Arkansas, and Pilgrim's Pride, which has one at Perkins, Arkansas.

71.4 JUNCTION SPUR – About 1910, a logging spur was built to the south to reach Dierks timber along the east side of the Saline River. In 1913, the mixed trains stopped here at what was called Junction Spur. By 1916, the location was known as Junction 21 as it was about 21 miles east of De Queen. There was once a wye here that served the logging line, which went south, crossed Messer Creek, and almost reached the Memphis, Dallas & Gulf Railroad; the Memphis, Paris & Gulf Railroad before June 1, 1910. To reach timber north of the mainline, a short spur track went as far as the Saline River, about a mile away.

Lines like this generally didn't last long as it would take only a season or two to cut the standing timber and ship it to a sawmill for processing. This logging line was still on the 1925 Arkansas Railroad Commission's Official Map. Maps from the 1930s no longer showed this line.

72.8 SHRUM SPRINGS – When the DeQueen & Eastern was being built to the east, newspaper reports stated that it "runs east by the Shrum springs." Railroad timetables during the 1910s showed a flag stop at Shrum Springs. During the 1920s, the railroad established a series of rates to and from Shrum Springs, including for grain, cement and lumber. The railroad's August 3, 1947, timetable listed a 4-car siding here. The station was still listed into the 1960s.

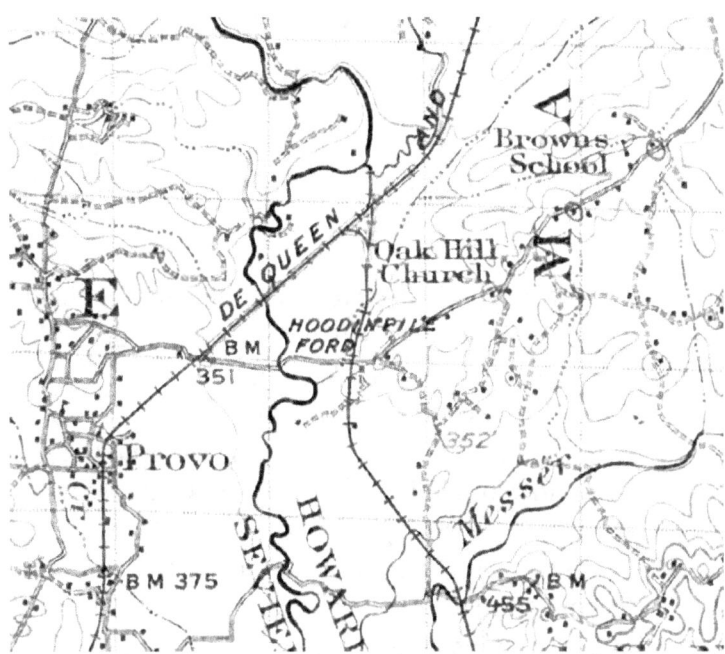

This map from 1913 shows the Dierks logging tracks that once left the DeQueen & Eastern Railroad at Milepost 71.4. United States Department of the Interior, Geological Survey, De Queen, AR, June 1913, Reprinted 1949. https://ngmdb.usgs.gov/ht-bin/tv_browse.pl?id=b34177bb7d4e8af355dca9d1bd88adbb

The station of Shrum Springs was located at the Allen Cemetery Road grade crossing. Members of the Shrum family settled in Possum Hollow, an area just south of Dierks, during the 1800s. Several members of the Shrum family are buried in the Allen Cemetery, located about a half-mile to the east.

74.0 BRIDGE – This 100-foot-long timber pile trestle crosses another small stream that drains the hills to the east and then flows into Holly Creek to the west. North of this bridge, the railroad curves to the east to reach Dierks. A benchmark at the bridge shows that the elevation is 385 feet.

74.6 WEST END DIERKS YARD LIMITS – Dierks is another station where switching takes place, plus the interchange between the local switcher and the Dierks Turn from De Queen. Because of this, it is protected by yard limits. This is the east end of the Track Warrant Control that started at Milepost 54.0.

75.0 HOLLY CREEK BRIDGE – The railroad finally crosses Holly Creek as it flows from the east. This timber pile trestle is 280 feet long.

Holly Creek forms in the hills less than 10 miles to the north. It flows south, and then around the east and south sides of Dierks. It then flows to the southwest before becoming a tributary of the Saline River. With Dierks siting in the valley of Holly Creek, the stream has historically been the cause of flooding in the community.

75.4 WEST END DIERKS COMPLEX – This is the west end of a series of yards and other tracks at Dierks, Arkansas. In this area there are four tracks, and yard limits are used to protect the operations. The rail complex is difficult to imagine as it has changed greatly over the past decade thanks to the closure of the pine veneer plant at Dierks in 2003 and the 2018 replacement of the original sawmill with a new one with a capacity to produce about 380 million board feet of lumber per year.

Despite the tracks curving from heading northeast to heading southeast at Dierks, the physical description of the railroad will continue to use east-west to simplify the information. Just east of the private road crossing at Milepost 75.4, the single-track mainline expands to be four tracks, all used for switching and building trains. These are long tracks that go as far east as Milepost 75.8, where the route goes back down to two tracks. At Milepost 76.2, the line has a short stretch of single track before tracks loop to the south into the old mill complex, and a short siding loops to the north. East of this area at Milepost 76.4 is a grade crossing with South Arkansas Avenue, the street that marks the west side of the old plywood and sawmill complex.

Heading east, the railroad crosses a small timber trestle (look for the Dierks station sign here) and then has a siding to the south begin, a track used for woodchip loading. At Milepost 76.9 is a grade crossing with the main entrance to the old mill, located at the south end of Herman Avenue. There is a short siding to the north of the mainline. The east end of all of these tracks come together at another private grade crossing for the old mill complex (Milepost 77.3). It is in this area that the track curves to the southeast. In the middle of this curve is a wooden pile trestle over Holly Creek. To the compass-east is the new pine mill.

There are several additional side tracks, one on each side of the mainline, that are used for loading woodchips, all west of a private grade crossing at Milepost 77.7. Just east of the crossing is a switch that brings all of the tracks back to a single main track. After experiencing another grade crossing with a private mill road at Milepost 77.8, the railroad has a switch that goes into the new mill complex to the northeast. This ends the Dierks complex of tracks.

During early 2023, the yard area at the west end of Dierks was stacked full of new railroad ties as the railroad was starting a major tie replacement project. This wall of ties was used to block access to part of the area.

The new ties stacked at Dierks created several unique photo opportunities, such as this one showing the Dierks Turn behind TO&E D-12 heading east into town.

76.5 DIERKS – The DeQueen & Eastern Railroad/Dierks Lumber & Coal built eight miles of track from Provo to the new town of Dierks in 1906. The first train arrived on Saturday, March 28, 1906, kicking off a celebration. A report from the *Arkansas Gazette* (April 3, 1906) reported that the "De Queen and Eastern Railroad has been built into Dierks, and the first train was run into the new town Saturday afternoon. The first engine that pulled a train into Dierks was No. 9, the oldest engine in service on the road. The event was celebrated by the continual blowing of whistles."

The railroad soon built a fine station at Dierks, described as being "a better station than any of the others except at De Queen." It was reportedly a "complete station which has the agent's quarters and white and black waiting room, and freight and express quarters." Management of the railroad stated that it had good platforms and the building was also in good condition. The 1907-1908 survey reported that the elevation of the top of rail in front of the Dierks station was 420.99 feet. The railroad also built a five-room section house at Dierks.

In 1909, Dierks was described as having a station, loading platform, warehouse, warehouse track, passing track, wye, and several spurs to logging camps. While lumber, logs, and crossties dominated the railroad shipments, there were other businesses that used the line at Dierks. Cotton, cotton seed, and livestock regularly were shipped over the DeQueen & Eastern. Elberta peaches were also canned at Dierks and then shipped on the railroad.

The railroad still marks its rail facilities at Dierks with this station sign, located near the main rail entrance of the old sawmill alongside U.S. Highway 70.

For years, the railroad maintained this depot at Dierks, Arkansas. It was still standing and well-maintained in 1989.

For five decades, Dierks was the east end of the timber holdings of Dierks, and was thus the east end of the DeQueen & Eastern Railroad. However, in 1957, Dierks spent $15 million to build a new kraft paper mill at Pine Bluff, Arkansas. Since much of the pulpwood and other raw materials would come from the territory along the DQ&E/TO&E, Dierks decided to extend its line eastward to make a connection with Missouri Pacific at the new station of Perkins. The plan was for the DQ&E to build to the southeast from Dierks and Missouri Pacific would build their line northward from Nashville.

Because Dierks was an important mill town and railroad terminal there have been a number of rail facilities and services here over the past century plus. These include a water tower, bulletin books, a train register station, a telephone station, a wye, and more. Minor repair work could be performed on the steam locomotives at the mill's shops. Many of these facilities were here because of the Harper Springs Logging Line, a Dierks Lumber operation that headed north from the mill.

Until the end of passenger service in 1948, Dierks was the east end of the railroad's passenger service. The railroad's station was on the north side of the DQ&E mainline at the south end of Main Street. In 1925, passenger train No. 2 arrived here at 7:30am daily except Sunday. It would turn at Dierks and depart at 8:45am as train No. 1. Towards the end of service in January 1945, a motorcar handled the service and arrived as train No. 6 at 2:10pm, operating daily except Sunday. The train would turn and depart as No. 7 at 3:40pm, arriving back at De Queen at 4:45pm.

Being at the east end of the railroad, there were a number of facilities at Dierks. The depot had a day telephone office, water station, and a 14-car siding in 1947. With the expansion of the railroad to Perkins, Dierks became the base of operations for switching the sawmill here, and the gypsum mill and interchange work to the east. The railroad still bases some train operations here, and interchanging cars between the train at Dierks and the Turn from De Queen is generally a weekday afternoon event. The wye tracks are gone today, but most of the yard tracks are still used almost daily.

DQ&E 4015 was assigned to the local switcher at Dierks during 2023. The locomotive is unique since it doesn't use the typical "D" designation.

DQ&E 4015 is switching cars as it passes the Dierks station sign.

The Dierks Switcher and the Dierks Turn are shown side-by-side at Dierks as they swap cars in 2023. Both of these locomotives show off the new Patriot Rail paint schemes.

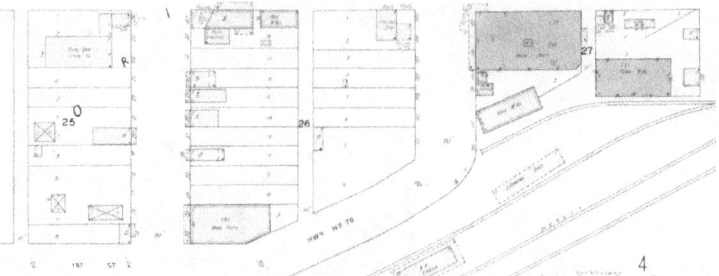

This 1937 map by the Sanborn Fire Insurance Map Company shows the location of the DeQueen & Eastern depot at Dierks, Arkansas. This area is now often used by trucks waiting for loading at the nearby sawmill. *Sanborn Fire Insurance Map from Dierks, Howard County, Arkansas.* Sanborn Map Company, August 1937. Map. Retrieved from the Library of Congress, https://www.loc.gov/item/sanborn00236_002/.

The Dierks Sawmill Complex

Most information about the City of Dierks starts with the various timber mills located in the community. At first, the area was simply a logging community. This changed in April 1908 when the company decided to install several small mills near Dierks to handle timber that had been downed by a recent storm. The plans were to haul the timber by railroad to Dierks to do any final cutting and sorting. Hardwood was an early subject of the cutting and the wood was used to manufacture items like barrel staves. As the hardwood was cut, the standing pine became the subject of the next series of plans by the company.

An article in the January 10, 1916, issue of *Lumber World Review* reported on plans by the Dierks Lumber & Coal Company to spend $250,000 to build a new pine sawmill at Dierks. It stated that Dierks owned "thousands of acres of very valuable timber lands in that vicinity, and has ordered a large tract near Dierks cleared off for the purpose of erecting the new plant thereon. Actual work on the mill plant will begin about February 1, and will be pushed to completion as fast as possible."

The double band sawmill went into operation during March 1918 and could produce about 135,000 board feet of lumber in 10 hours. To prepare the lumber for market, the cut and sized lumber was put through fourteen reinforced concrete National dry kilns, with a daily kiln capacity of 250,000 feet. There was also an electrically operated 20-ton ice plant at Dierks.

An inspection report by the Sanborn Fire Insurance Map Company provided additional information about the mill. It reported that the mill had a capacity of 200,000 board feet per day, it had an inventory stock of 2 million board feet (none piled in yards but instead stored in dry sheds), and that there was sufficient uncut timber in the vicinity to supply the mill for 6 to 10 years. The mill was big and busy, and it employed about 500 men.

The December 25, 1920, issue of *American Lumberman* provided a report on the mill at Dierks.

The Dierks plant being the newest as well as the largest of the company's four mills, a somewhat detailed description will be of general interest. The plant which has a capacity of 135,000 feet per day of ten hours, was built and equipped for night and day shifts although it never as yet has been run nights. About five hundred men are employed in the Dierks woods operation and the mill. The log pond covers about five acres and has capacity for 1,500,000 feet of logs.

> *The plant at Dierks is equipped with two Fil-er & Stowell 9-foot band mills, with 14-inch saws. It has a double 72-inch edger and an Al-lis-Chalmers air lift trimmer. All the machin-ery, both in the sawmill and the planing mill, is driven by electric power, there being a total of sixty-eight motors, ranging from one to 250 horsepower.*

As the sawmill was being built, Dierks started ac-quiring trucks to haul their timber from the woods. This was done because of a tornado that tore a 20-mile route through their woods, and the time required to build rail lines was too long to salvage some of the timber. A report on the experiment was published in *Lumber World Review* (August 25, 1919). This test led the company to stop building local logging lines, and to instead only build major branches and use trucks to get the timber to the tracks.

While rebuilt and modernized several times, the pine mill remained at Dierks for a century. During September 1969, Weyerhaeuser Company acquired Dierks Forest Inc., for $192,000,000. This included the mills, railroads, and timberlands. With a nation-al network, Weyerhaeuser had duplicate facilities and worked to modernize some and close others. In September 2003, Weyerhaeuser moved the pro-duction of pine veneer from Dierks to its plywood plants at Mountain Pine, Arkansas, and Wright City, Oklahoma. As stated by the company, this would allow Dierks to focus on lumber and move the ply-wood production to more efficient operations. At the time, the Dierks plant could produce 150 million square feet of veneer annually, while the company had a total of 14 plants producing 2.8 billion square feet of plywood and veneer annually. Thus, this plant produced only about 5% of the company's total volume each year.

The importance of the pine mill was demonstrated a decade later when plans were announced in 2015 to construct an upgraded facility to replace the former pine mill. Weyerhaeuser spent $190 million to upgrade the facility, which could produce about 380 million board feet of lumber per year. The new mill opened during October 2018. Today, the mill produces large volumes of pine timber and carloads of woodchips for paper production.

Parts of the original Dierks sawmill complex were built of concrete, and because of this, many parts still stand abandoned where they were originally built.

Because of the construction of a new sawmill, and the closure of the old mill, there are a number of abandoned tracks at Dierks.

This Weyerhaeuser Dierks Lumber sign marks the entrance to the new mill on the east side of town.

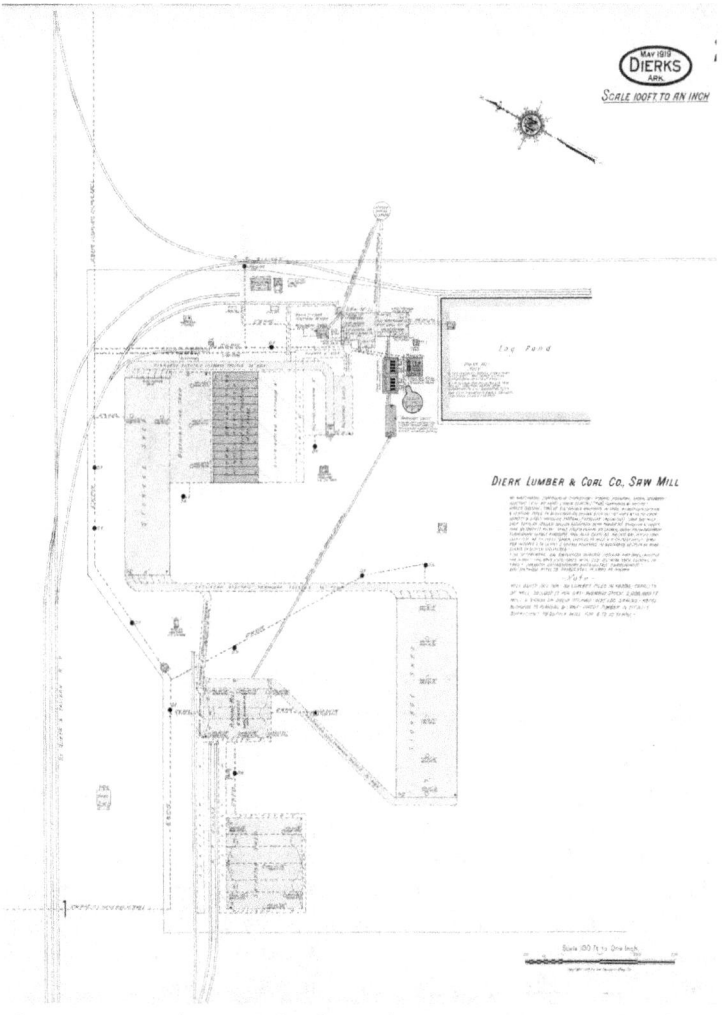

This map, created in 1919 by the Sanborn Fire Insurance Map Company, shows the large Dierks mill complex at Dierks, Arkansas. Note all of the tracks of the DeQueen & Eastern Railroad on the north and east sides of the mill. *Sanborn Fire Insurance Map from Dierks, Howard County, Arkansas.* Sanborn Map Company, May, 1919. Map. Retrieved from the Library of Congress, https://www.loc.gov/item/sanborn00236_001/.

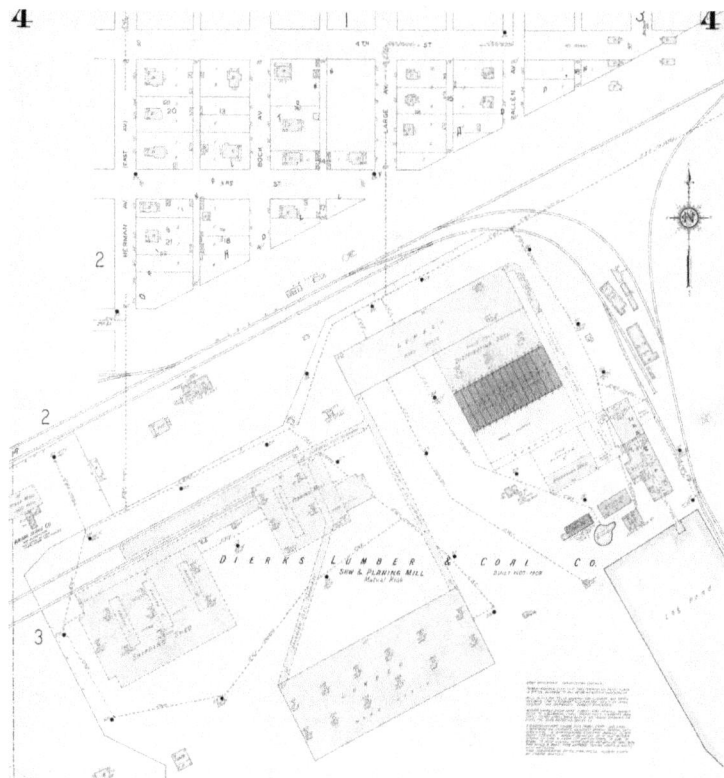

This map, created in 1937 by the Sanborn Fire Insurance Map Company, shows the large Dierks mill complex at Dierks, Arkansas. Note all of the tracks of the DeQueen & Eastern Railroad on the north and east sides of the mill, and the minor changes made at the mil during the previous decade. *Sanborn Fire Insurance Map from Dierks, Howard County, Arkansas.* Sanborn Map Company, August 1937. Retrieved from the Library of Congress https://www.loc.gov/item/sanborn00236_002/.

The Harper Springs Logging Line

Reports about short logging lines out of Dierks started soon after the DeQueen & Eastern reached the community. One of the earliest was a report from December 1909 that the railroad had built 12 miles of railroad from Dierks to a place called Beyond. By 1912, a government survey report noted that a benchmark was located 1.8 miles north of Dierks "along old tramway now used as wagon road." A 1917 government report about the region noted that there were two logging lines heading out of Dierks. One headed to the southeast and followed Little Holly Creek for about a half-dozen miles. The second logging line headed south and crossed Messer Creek, about six miles away. In April 1921, Spur 100 was shown to serve as a logging line out of Dierks.

However, the most documented logging line stretched north from Dierks, heading more than a reported 50 miles to near the Saline River. This line went to a logging camp named Harper Springs Camp, located at the extreme northern edge of Howard County. Reports from the time stated that the company town had as many as 500 residents, and it had a post office from 1925 until 1931. There was also a Harper Springs school and several businesses.

The rail line to Harper Springs was built by Dierks Lumber & Coal during the mid-1920s, and its purpose was to move logs to the mill at Dierks. As the line opened, Dierks received several steam locomotives, such as #227 which is on display at Broken Bow, Oklahoma. This steam locomotive was built by Baldwin in May 1927 and was first assigned to this line.

Harper Springs Camp or Harper Camp was the base of logging operations on the logging line. In 1925, officials of Dierks Lumber & Coal requested the establishment of a post office at Harper Camp. It was originally located in the extreme northeast corner of Sevier County, ½ mile west of the Saline River and ¼ mile north of Panther Creek near Thompson Ford. Postal reports stated that the location was 30 miles northwest from Dierks using existing roads, and that the Harper Camp post office would be 100 feet south of the tracks of the Dierks Lumber Company Log Railroad. In 1927, the post office moved 1.2 miles to the northeast and into Howard County with Hazel E. Brenson serving as postmaster. The site is now under the waters of Dierks Lake.

With just a few short hikes, a traveler could have taken a train over this route, connected to other logging lines in the Ouachita hills, and wound up at either Mena or Fort Smith, Arkansas. Nearly every hollow or river valley was being logged by temporary rail lines. However, the various Dierks operations outlasted them all.

With the sawmill at Dierks, plus a number of different logging lines over the years, Dierks Lumber & Coal assigned a number of locomotives and other rail equipment to Dierks, Arkansas. This photo from the December 25, 1920, issue of the *American Lumberman* shows the Dierks service track, which housed several steam locomotives and a log loader.

In 1930, the Harper Springs Camp won the annual Dierks safety award when 426 men worked 597,455 hours without a major injury. However, the efficiency of the workers led to the timber being cut, and the Great Depression reduced the demand for the timber. The post office closed in 1931 as Dierks shut down many of their operations at Harper Springs, although some documents state that parts of the line lasted until as late as 1954.

History of Dierks, Arkansas

Dierks, Arkansas, was the destination of the railroad heading east due to the large acreage of standing timber that had been acquired by the lumber company. The first train arrived here on March 28, 1906, and a report in the *Arkansas Gazette* (June 28, 1906) stated that the Town of Dierks had been surveyed and located on March 1, 1906. Apparently part of the town had been built before the railroad arrived and the townsite surveyed, and it had grown quickly after it became official. The news article stated that the depot had been built, a bank had opened, there was a newspaper (*The Dierks News*), two hotels, four mercantile stores, and two restaurants. It also reported that a Baptist church was under construction.

The Dierks' logging town wasn't the first community in the area. Settlers had arrived here and cleared land for farms by 1848. At the time, the area was described as being a dense forest of pine, oak, and hickory trees. The community acquired the name Hardscrabble, and it was connected to the county seat by a poor wagon road which headed southward 8 miles to Center Point. Center Point lost its title of county seat in 1884 when it was moved to Nashville, which had just received a railroad thanks to a predecessor of the Missouri Pacific Railroad. Despite the dense woods, farming became the main economic activity, with cotton being very important.

Things changed with the appearance of the Dierks brothers, and the standing timber became a resource, not a challenge. During the early 1900s, Dierks Lumber & Coal bought much of the standing timber, and the population of Hardscrabble grew due to the lumbering activity. When the town was chosen to be essentially a company town for the logging firm, it was renamed for Hans Dierks, the oldest of the brothers who co-owned the company. The arrival of the railroad in early 1906 led to the creation of a post office and a public school that year.

Advertisements like this encouraged the development of the town of Dierks. *Mena Weekly Star.* Mena, AR, March 8, 1917, p. 4. Retrieved from the Library of Congress, www.loc.gov/item/sn89051213/1917-03-08/ed-1/.

The city incorporated on June 4, 1907, and John William Pate opened a bottling company in Dierks to produce fruit-flavored sodas the same year. The company started to bottle Coca-Cola in 1910. The population in the census that year was 272, but after the pine sawmill was built, the 1920 census recorded a population of 1495, thanks to the more than 500 workers at the mill. Cotton was still important at the time as the Cook & Price cotton gin was located a block to the west of the depot in 1919. It later became the Dierks Gin Company, and was located where a modern gas station now sits. There were a number of private business in Dierks – movie theaters, restaurants, hotels, dry cleaning, auto sales and repair, clothing, and the grist mill and shingle mill of H. D. Watson & Son. However, the Dierks Lumber & Coal Company also had their "Big Store" which had a selection of almost anything someone would want.

At one time, Dierks was very close to being a company town, with most of it consisting of company houses and sawmill. A few signs of this era still remain, such as this house, one of several identical structures that still stand.

During World War I, due to a shortage of labor, the lumber company built a second community at Dierks to house black workers and their families. This neighborhood featured its own hotel, two churches, a school, and stores. This community was located south of the tracks and on the west side of the mill, along what is today South Arkansas Avenue. Nothing remains of this neighborhood.

The 1930 census recorded the highest official population ever with 1544 residents. The population has been on a fairly steady decline ever since, mainly due to the use of machinery in the woods and at the mill. The end of cotton farming also had an impact on the families in the area. The Great Depression hurt the community, as it did everywhere, but Dierks Lumber was able to keep much of the business going. Additionally, the Works Projects Administration (WPA) made improvements to the town, and the Civilian Conservation Corps (CCC) established a 200-worker camp near Dierks in 1933. For two years, these workers controlled forest fires and worked to preserve and improve forested areas.

During World War II, the first women were hired to fill positions in the mill, working as planers, craters, and shippers. The presence of the mill brought many workers back after the war, and the community stabilized at a population of about 1200 until the loss of the plywood mill in 2003. Since then, the population has dropped until only 916 residents were reported in the 2020 census. Despite this, the town still features its own school system, post office, churches, several banks, restaurants, gas stations, and a number of other businesses. The modern sawmill stands over the southeast part of town, and the community still holds its annual Pine Tree Festival the first weekend in August.

79.2 EAST END DIERKS YARD LIMITS – Located a short distance west of Tram Road is the east end of the Dierks yard limits and the west end of the former Perkins Block. On August 17, 2017, the railroad changed its operating control system from using Block Register Territory to Track Warrant Control. The railroad changed back to block limits a few years later, and then during early 2023 converted to using track warrant control.

This sign marks the start of the Perkins Block at the east end of the Dierks Yard Limits.

79.5 U.S. HIGHWAY 278 – The railroad crosses this 1074-mile-long highway at grade. Running parallel to U.S. Highway 78, this road heads east from Wickes, Arkansas, to Hilton Head Island, South Carolina.

Just west of Highway 278 is a grade crossing with Old Tram Road. U.S. Geological Survey maps from 1906 and 1913 show a rail line heading southeast out of Dierks. It followed the Little Holly Creek to this area and was used for logging.

East of Dierks is a grade crossing with Old Tram Road, named for an early logging line along the route.

85.1 WEST END PERKINS YARD LIMITS – The tracks used to serve the gypsum mill at Briar, and the nearby Perkins Yard, are all protected by yard limits which start here and head east to Milepost 86.6.

85.3 BRIAR CREEK BRIDGE – A timber pile trestle is used to cross this small stream, which provides the railroad name for this area. Briar Creek forms in the hills to the south and flows northward, eventually into Muddy Fork.

85.4 ARKANSAS HIGHWAY 369 – The Arkansas State Highway Commission created Highway 369 on January 12, 1966, and it has been expanded by adding several very short sections in 1978 and 1980. The route connects Nashville, Arkansas, with the Albert Pike Recreation Area north of Langley, Arkansas. The highway shares its route in several places, technically making the roadway a series of sections.

There is a switch immediately to the east of the grade crossing. This is the beginning of the series of tracks at Briar.

85.6 BRIAR WYE – To the north is a short siding and a wye track. Each leg of the wye can hold about ten freight cars, and the tail of the wye is just long enough to hold several locomotives.

This photo from the shoulder of Arkansas Highway 369 shows the area around the west wye switch at Briar, Arkansas.

When the DeQueen & Eastern was extended eastward, several surprises were found near the old community of Briar. First, a number of beds of gypsum were found, with an aggregate thickness of as much as twenty feet. This gypsum created a new industry in the area. A second discovery was found while mining the gypsum. In 1983, a series of dinosaur tracks were found at the Briar gypsum quarry. The first found were sauropod tracks, made by an enormous animal with a long neck and tail, a small head, and four thick, pillar-like legs. Other types of dinosaur tracks have also been found, including tridactyl in 2011.

86.0 CERTAINTEED SWITCH – Just east of the Briar Road grade crossing is a switch to a long track that is used to serve the CertainTeed gypsum plant. A chance discovery of gypsum deposits during the construction of the rail line through here in 1956 led to the station of Briar. A few years later a large mill was built at Briar to use the material by making gypsum wallboard.

This sign marks the highway entrance into the CertainTeed gypsum plant at Perkins, Arkansas. This mill is the easternmost shipper on the DeQueen & Eastern Railroad.

The mill has been through a number of owners. Dierks Forests, Inc., opened the plant in 1963. When created, this plant was one of the world's ten largest producers of wallboard. With the sale of the company, the plant became owned by Weyerhaeuser Company. Since then, it has been owned by James Hardie Gypsum, Boral, BPB Gypsum, and currently CertainTeed Company, a wholly owned subsidiary of Saint Gobain. Saint Gobain is a major international company with world markets in construction products and materials, as well as packaging. CertainTeed was founded in 1904 as General Roofing

Manufacturing Company, and still produces roofing, siding, fence, decking, railing, trim, insulation, gypsum and ceilings.

Heading east on the DeQueen & Eastern Railroad, the tracks are actually heading south.

During the railroad's centennial event in 2000, the railroad performed this photo runby for its passengers at Milepost 86.0.

86.8   WEST SWITCH OF PERKINS YARD – Perkins Yard includes four tracks. The west switch is located immediately north of a grade crossing with a haul road used for moving gypsum from a quarry to the west to the CertainTeed plant to the east. A series of quarries can be found in this area, some still active and some filled with water. At least one is used as a landfill, with a road crossing at Union Pacific Milepost 492, which is 1.3 miles south of here.

This CertainTeed Gypsum Mine Sign protects the road that crosses the tracks at the west end of Perkins Yard. This area is clearly marked as private and trespassing is not tolerated.

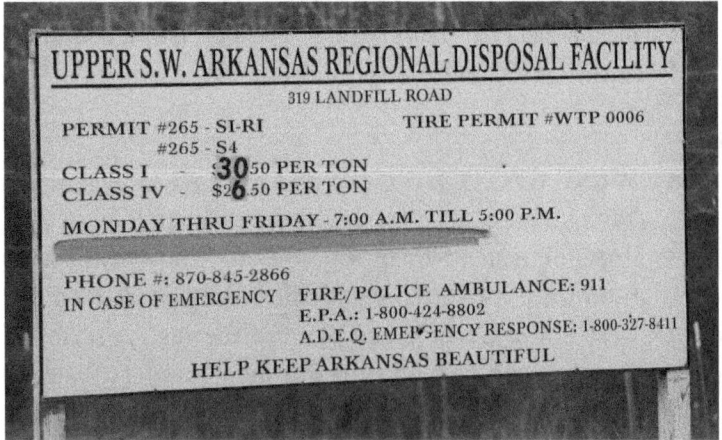

This sign shows that some of the old gypsum quarries are now used as landfills. This road crosses the Union Pacific tracks just south of the Perkins Yard.

87.0 **PERKINS** – This is the east end of the DeQueen & Eastern Railroad, and the beginning of the Nashville Subdivision of Union Pacific. This creates the mileage conversion of DQ&E Milepost 87.0 = UP Milepost 493.1. The Union Pacific line continues on through Nashville to Hope and a connection with UP's St. Louis-Little Rock-Dallas mainline.

Historically, a "dodger" would operate from Dierks to Perkins and back, handling the switching at Perkins. A dodger is a term for a local freight train, a name borrowed from the Kansas City Southern. At Dierks, the Dierks-Perkins Dodger would interchange traffic with a train out of De Queen. This allowed trains to serve the customers along the line and move freight across the railroad, but keep the crews within the hours of service requirements. Because the train from Dierks would turn at Perkins, a small office with a train register was kept here.

The extension of both railroads to Perkins started with plans for a new kraft paper mill at Pine Bluff, Arkansas. Dierks would own the mill and supply many of the raw materials from their operations along the DeQueen & Eastern/Texas, Oklahoma & Eastern. One potential route was to use the Kansas City Southern to deliver loads to Missouri Pacific, but using a long route with three railroads would take too long and was determined to be too expensive. Dierks decided to extend its line eastward to make a connection with Missouri Pacific at the new station of Perkins. The plan was for the DQ&E to build to the southeast from Dierks and Missouri Pacific would build their line northward from Nashville. This would provide a shorter two-railroad route for the carloads of chips, sawdust, and other products.

The Interstate Commerce Commission gave authority for the line's construction on February 27, 1956, with the provisions that work was to begin by April 5, 1956, and that the work would be finished by February 15, 1957. Clearing of the route soon began to comply with the requirements. The line between the two railroads opened at 9:30am on January 19, 1957. Perkins was simply the midpoint of the construction. Missouri Pacific built the 10-mile line from Nashville to here, spending a reported $500,000, and provided the rail for the DeQueen & Eastern and their 10 miles of line, costing approximately $200,000. When the line opened, each railroad ran a passenger special to here with the two company presidents, Fred H. Dierks (President of Dierks Forests) and Paul J. Neff (President of Missouri Pacific), each planning to drive a golden spike. However, the cold dampness of the morning seemed to have changed the plans as a gasoline-powered spiking machine was used instead. The location was named Perkins after Charles E. Perkins, former chief traffic officer of the Missouri Pacific.

The name Perkins was actually once a common one in the area. Isaac Cooper Perkins, a farmer and Baptist missionary, was the first to settle where Nashville eventually developed. Perkins had built a cabin in the area in the 1820s, and he finally obtained his first official land grant in 1836. He was joined by his wife and five daughters, and then became a traveling preacher who served congregations from Little Rock, Arkansas, to Jefferson, Texas. He was able to obtain more land grants in the Nashville and surrounding areas, and became one of the leaders as the region developed.

This new Pilgrim Feed Mill was built just south of Perkins Yard on the tracks of Union Pacific. This mill replaced the older mill in downtown Nashville, Arkansas.

Union Pacific Nashville Subdivision

The track from Perkins south belongs to Union Pacific Railroad. Construction on the line started with 9 miles of track built in 1879 by the Washington & Hope Railway. Connecting the two towns in its name, the railroad was originally built using wooden rail and to a gauge of 3 feet, and used horses and mule power. In 1880, the wooden rails and livestock were replaced by iron and steam locomotives, and the next year the railroad was rebuilt to standard gauge. The line was extended 16 miles in 1884 when the Arkansas & Louisiana Railway built the line to Nashville.

The St. Louis, Iron Mountain & Southern Railway Company acquired the property on September 1, 1909. On August 19, 1915, both the Iron Mountain and the Missouri Pacific Railway Company entered receivership. The two railroads were sold at foreclosure to the creditors of the lines on February 21, 1917. Most of the two systems were then merged into the new Missouri Pacific Railroad Company on May 12, 1917.

During 1927, the Missouri Pacific Railroad extended the line 7.5 miles to near Perkins. At the time, this extension was known as the Nashville Peach Spur as it was built to serve the peach-growing area north of Nashville. This construction was spurred on by the shipment of 250,000 bushels of peaches from the Nashville area in 1925. The new line would serve at least four large fruit operations and their orchards: Reeder, Big Four, Roberson, and the Home Orchard Company. At the same time, there was talk about the line being extended to connect to the Prescott & Northwestern near Corinth, Arkansas.

In 1950, most of this extension was abandoned after receiving approval from the Interstate Commerce Commission on May 31, 1950. Although the line was still used by some shippers, continuing losses forced the railroad to abandon the line. The timing was good as in 1952 and 1953, late freezes followed early warm spells, destroying about two-thirds of the peach crop and killing many of the trees. The peach industry in the area never recovered.

However, in 1956, the abandoned line was rebuilt and extended to create a junction with the DeQueen & Eastern at Perkins. Missouri Pacific would provide a route for shipments to the new Dierks paper mill at Pine Bluff, Arkansas, justifying the construction of the line. An interesting part of this construction was that Missouri Pacific had to buy a right-of-way through the forests of Dierks so it could haul the forest products of Dierks.

On January 8, 1980, the Union Pacific Corporation announced an agreement to buy the Missouri Pacific Railroad, or merge as often stated. Approval was finally received on September 13, 1982, after a series of hearings and lawsuits. It finally took a Supreme Court ruling to allow the merger on December 22, 1982. A unique detail not known by many was that the Missouri Pacific had a number of outstanding bonds that prevented a full merger of the two companies. The bonds were finally closed during the mid-1990s, and the merger became final on January 1, 1997. Today, the Union Pacific line is the Nashville Subdivision which extends 35.6 miles from Hope to Perkins. The end of UP ownership is at their Milepost 493.1, at an elevation of 542 feet.

Union Pacific's Nashville Subdivision is named for Nashville, Arkansas. This worn station sign can be found at Milepost 483 at Nashville, less than ten miles south of the interchange yard at Perkins.

The Other Dierks Railroads

The DeQueen & Eastern and the Texas, Oklahoma & Eastern are unique among the various railroads created, built and operated by the Dierks Lumber & Coal Company and its associated companies as they still exist. Many of the Dierks railroads were built to move timber to mills and lumber to market, and they lasted only as long as the timber remained. Many of these lines were big, like the Clebit Logging Line out of Wright City, a line that was more than fifty miles long when its major logging branches are included. The Harper Springs Logging Line at Dierks was also once about the same length. Basic information about these rail lines is included in the route guide information for the DeQueen & Eastern.

However, not all of these Dierks railroads branched off of the Valliant to Perkins mainline. Others could be found in Louisiana, Texas, Oklahoma and Arkansas, and there were a number that were planned but never built. Some of these rail lines were originally built by other companies and were later acquired by Dierks Lumber & Coal, or at least members of the Dierks family. Other lines were built as partnerships or even solely for Dierks Lumber. The largest of these Dierks-related railroad operations are covered here.

Sabine & Eastern Railway

The Dierks Lumber & Coal Company purchased the N. A. Ayers Lumber Company of Florien, Louisiana, in 1906, renaming it the Florien Lumber Company. Herman Dierks served as the company's president. John S. Kirkpatrick (ex-Supreme Court Justice of Nebraska) served as the company's attorney, just as he did for the DeQueen & Eastern. *The St. Louis Lumberman* of April 1, 1908, reported that the "Florien Lumber Company of Ayres, La., had recently built and equipped a new mill which will be ready to operate within the next two weeks." It was also stated that the Dierks Lumber & Coal Company of Kansas City owned the controlling interest in the lumber company.

The lumber company had its own railroad, the Sabine & Eastern Railway Company. It was shown to operate from the Florien Lumber Company southern pine mill at Ayers (Sabine Parish), for about five miles into the nearby timber. Florien Lumber shipped its finished lumber on the Kansas City Southern Railway from Ayers, receiving a share of the freight rate. In 1910, the Louisiana Railroad Commission called the railroad a logging line, and it gave the Kansas City Southern authority to install a gate at the crossing between the two railroads, located about a mile south of Florien. This gate eliminated the need for KCS trains to stop before going over the crossing. At this time, the Sabine & Eastern showed that it hauled freight but received no revenue from hauling passengers.

By 1913, the railroad was shown to be eight miles long and used 35-pound and 45-pound rail. The standard gauge railroad used two locomotives and 15 log cars, and the lumber company operated its own commissary store. Among the steam locomotives was former DeQueen & Eastern RR #100, a Class B45-2 Shay built in July 1903 for the Dierks Lumber & Coal Company.

Nearby Florien had received a post office in 1897, but Ayers didn't receive a post office until 1907 when Dierks Lumber acquired the local lumber company. It didn't last long as the community of Ayers closed down, the post office closed in 1912, and Florien Lumber was liquidated in 1913. The railroad was also quickly removed.

Waterman Lumber & Supply Company Railways

This Texas lumber company, along with its logging and tap line, started as the W. M. Waterman Lumber Company in 1905. Founded by William Madison Waterman, often cited as being a German emigrant , the company actually dated to 1901 when Waterman completed a sawmill of 40,000 feet daily capacity at Timpson, Texas. To get the lumber to market, Waterman was instrumental in organizing the Texas & Gulf Railroad (T&G) in 1904, which acquired the Texas, Sabine Valley & Northwestern Railway Company; Marshall, Timpson & Sabine Pass Railway Company; and Texas & Sabine Valley Railway Company on December 27, 1904. Over the next several years, the T&G extended the line from Timpson to Grigsby (1905-1907) and Gary to Center (1907-1909). With the railroad's expansion, Waterman Lumber & Supply Company shipped from Timpson and Waterman on the Texas & Gulf Railway. The Atchison, Topeka & Santa Fe Railway eventually acquired control of the Texas & Gulf through its Gulf, Colorado & Santa Fe Railway subsidiary.

On June 21, 1905, the Waterman Lumber & Supply Company was created by a partnership between the W. M. Waterman Lumber Company and the Dierks Lumber & Coal Company. In 1908, the company built a second mill, "located sixteen miles south of Timpson and connected to it by the company tap-line and logging tram road." The April 1, 1908, issue of *The St. Louis Lumberman* reported that the new Waterman Lumber & Supply Company sawmill at Waterman was finished and the machinery was being placed. It was also reported that the mill would have a capacity of about 100,000 feet of yellow and southern pine per day. About this time, Hans Dierks was president of the firm, which operated three sawmills and a tap line and logging railroad.

In May 1909, *The St. Louis Lumberman* reported that a new plant was being completed at Waterman that was owned jointly by the Ingham Lumber Company and the Dierks Lumber & Coal Company. The new plant had a daily capacity of 150,000 feet of yellow pine, and included a planing mill and dry kilns. The new lumber town of Waterman also included about 200 tenant homes, a union church, segregated company commissaries, a large hotel, a post office, depot, barber shop, and a drug store.

Texas records show that the Waterman Lumber & Supply Company's incorporation ended on June 21, 1915. By that year, the operation was generally called Dierks Lumber & Coal Company, even though Waterman was still serving as the firm's superintendent. The company shipped most of its lumber to the Dierks lumberyards in Nebraska until more mills opened in Arkansas and Oklahoma. Then, the output of the Waterman Lumber & Supply Company went to Europe until those markets were cut off during the First World War.

A sign that the company was cleaning up the last of the timber was that it was advertising that it was cutting yellow pine, cypress, oak, gum, hickory, ash, walnut, and cottonwood. In 1920, the operation's properties were sold off, with Frost Industries of Nacogdoches buying much of the land, as well as the sawmill as Waskom, Texas.

The various mills of the Waterman operations were connected by several rail lines. Two Shay locomotives were used primarily on the logging lines. Waterman Lumber & Supply #1 (Class B28-2) was actually built in 1907 for the R. G. Andrews Lumber Company and later sold to Waterman. Waterman Lumber & Supply #2 (Class B37-2) was built for Waterman in late 1906. At least three of the Baldwin Prairie-type (2-6-2) steam locomotives associated with Dierks also operated on the railroads of the Waterman Lumber & Supply Company. The first was DeQueen & Eastern #200, which was moved to Waterman in 1910. In 1912, two similar locomotives were built, one for the Texas, Oklahoma & Eastern (#203) and one for the Waterman Lumber & Supply Company (#204). All of these 2-6-2 locomotives moved about the various Dierks properties over the next several decades.

The logging railroads generally hauled the workers to and from the woods each day, but this led to several major accidents. A derailment on February 11, 1907, resulted in the death of one Waterman Lumber Company laborer. The news report stated that trains of the Texas & Gulf Railway Company also operated over this track. Another derailment in September 1911 resulted in the song *The Waterman Train Wreck*. Some of the lines of the song tell the story.

> *September, Friday morning,*
> *this lonesome train did come,*
> *Out into the pine woods, it was our daily run.*
> *But on our trip returning, a tragedy occurred,*
> *The train derailed with four men killed,*
> *distress is what we heard.*

> *That fateful autumn morning,*
> *the year nineteen-eleven,*
> *Four men who rode that steaming train*
> *took their final run to heaven.*
> *We heard the cries in Waterman,*
> *it broke our hearts to hear,*
> *The wailing wives and sweethearts,*
> *they faced their deepest fear.*

The railroads of the Waterman Lumber & Supply Company were scattered over the Shelby and Harrison county areas of northeast Texas. These were generally shown to be standard gauge. The lines out of Waterman operated 1907 to at least 1917 and the mileage varied between 4 and 30 miles. A line at Blocker operated between 1910 and 1917 and the mileage varied between 12 and 19 miles. At Waskom, a series of logging lines operated during the late 1910s and early 1920s. When the operations were investigated as part of the Tap Line cases. J. S. Kirkpatrick represented Waterman Lumber & Supply, Dierks Lumber & Coal, Ingham Lumber, and Florien Lumber, showing their close relationships. Kirkpatrick was an associate of the Dierks, and once served as a justice on the Nebraska Supreme Court.

TOTAL DAILY PRODUCTION 58 CARS.

DIERKS, ARK.
PINE DAILY PRODUCTION 15 CARS.

BISMARK, OKLA.
PINE DAILY PRODUCTION 15 CARS.

BROKEN BOW, OKLA.
PINE DAILY PRODUCTION 8 CARS.
HARDWOOD DAILY PRODUCTION 7 CARS.

WATERMAN, TEX.
PINE DAILY PRODUCTION 6 CARS.

DE QUEEN, ARK.
PINE DAILY PRODUCTION 4 CARS.

PACKARD, ARK.
PINE DAILY PRODUCTION 3 CARS.

In 1921, the stationary of Dierks Lumber & Coal listed the production capacity of its various sawmills. Among those listed was Waterman, Texas, with a daily capacity of 6 carloads of pine lumber.

Oklahoma & Rich Mountain Railroad

Probably the most documented of these other Dierks railroads is the Oklahoma & Rich Mountain Railroad Company. This railroad was located on the Kansas City Southern 80 miles north of De Queen at Page, Oklahoma. The Oklahoma & Rich Mountain (O&RM) was incorporated under the General Laws of Oklahoma on September 28, 1925, with the stated purpose to construct, own and operate a line of railroad from a connection with the Kansas City Southern Railway Company at Page, Oklahoma, to a connection with the Frisco Railway Company at Talihina, Oklahoma. Records show that the O&RM was organized on October 1, 1925, and almost immediately applied to the Interstate Commerce Commission (ICC) for permission to build the railroad.

On February 18, 1926, the ICC approved building the railroad, with the conditions that "the construction of said line of railroad shall be commenced on or before July 1, 1926, and be completed on or before December 31, 1927." The ICC hearing produced a large amount of information about the plans for the railroad, including that the St Louis-San Francisco Railway Company and the Kansas City Southern Railway Company stated that the proposed line was "necessary to develop a territory not now served by any carrier, especially for the marketing of lumber, and that it will furnish additional business to them as connecting carriers." The territory where the railroad was to be built included timberlands (75%), pasture (15%), and land under cultivation (10%). The level land and the river and creek valleys were claimed to be good farm lands, while the rough and mountainous portions were mostly covered with a virgin growth of timber. It was estimated by the O&RM that there was sufficient timber to permit the operation of a large lumber plant for 20 to 25 years. It was also stated that the owners of the timberlands would probably reforest, so that the lumber industry could be maintained almost indefinitely.

The railroad was to be standard gauge, single track, and laid with 60-pound rail. The rail would be "leased from the Kansas City Southern on a rental basis of 6 per cent per annum on a valuation of $23 per ton." The estimated maximum grade of the railroad was 2 percent, and the maximum curvature was estimated at 10 degrees. The railroad would use the station of the Kansas City Southern at Page, paying as rental 1.25 percent on its valuation and 25 percent of the expense of operating it. There were also proposed stations at Muse, 16 miles west of Page, and at Talihina, the western terminus at the Frisco's Central Division line.

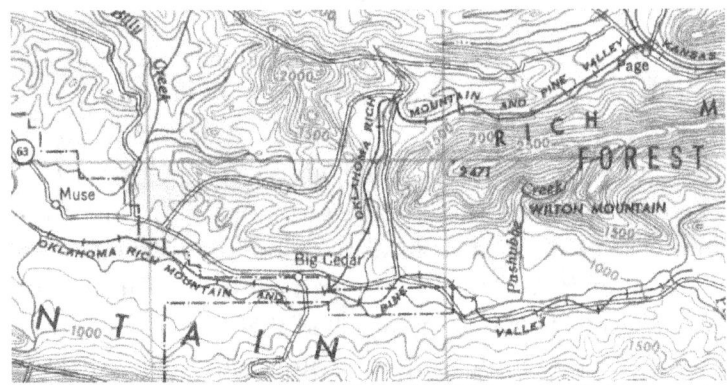

Despite being abandoned in late 1941, the Oklahoma & Rich Mountain Railroad was still shown on this 1950 topo map. Note that it was shown to be the Oklahoma, Rich Mountain & Pine Valley. *Topo Map, Oklahoma - 1950, printed 8-1951.* Chief of Engineers, Corps of Engineers, U.S. Army Map Service, McAlister, OK. https://ngmdb.usgs.gov/ht-bin/tv_browse.pl?id=9eea739440748667b6bcdae4a6955608

Traffic from forest products for the first year of operation was estimated at 2000 carloads, increasing to 2500 carloads the second year, and remaining constant for the three years following. Products of agriculture were expected to provide a traffic of 100 carloads the first year, increasing to 200 carloads the fifth year. Traffic from livestock and miscellaneous was estimated at 105 carloads the first year and 160 carloads the fifth year. To handle the timber business, Dierks created the Pine Valley Lumber Company, a company described as being organized by and operated in the interests of the Dierks Lumber & Coal Company. The board of the Oklahoma & Rich Mountain Railroad consisted of members from the boards of the DeQueen & Eastern and the Texas, Oklahoma & Eastern. The various rail operations provided the steam locomotives and freight cars used on the O&RM.

The Dierks family had close ties with the management of the Kansas City Southern (KCS), and even before construction began it had a special rate for moving lumber off of the line. Because of this, only seventeen miles of railroad from the KCS at Page were built, never reaching the Frisco at Talihina. Construction on the line reportedly began even before the ICC approved the plan, with the initial work conducted by the Dierks Lumber & Coal Company. The railroad reportedly opened for operations on October 11, 1928, to Pine Valley, Oklahoma. The Pine Valley area had been settled by 1896 and was known as Muse. However, the Pine Valley Lumber Company renamed the community on December 16, 1926. when it was developed as a lumber milling and logging community. A new nearby community of Muse was created a year later.

When completed, the Oklahoma & Rich Mountain used 0.58 miles of sidings and station facilities at Page, owned by the Kansas City Southern. The line then headed west following a small stream up into the mountains, where it turned to the south to Big Cedar. Here, the railroad turned to the west to reach Pine Valley. A short branch headed to the east to reach timber along the Kiamichi River. In total, the Page-Pine Valley mainline measured 16.946 miles, and there were 1.216 miles of yard tracks and sidings. At Pine Valley, the O&RM used part of a warehouse that was owned by the Pine Valley Lumber Company as its station.

Lumber was the primary product moved on the railroad, especially during the first few years of the company. The only significant town along the railroad was Pine Valley, which had a population of about 1500. The town featured company housing, a company commissary, schools and churches, and even a movie theater. The town also had electricity and treated drinking water. For a short time during the early 1930s, the mill at Pine Valley was the only Dierks operation producing lumber, and officially became part of Dierks Lumber in 1936. For the year 1939, the Interstate Commerce Commission reported that the Oklahoma & Rich Mountain made $41,847 hauling freight, $2059 moving mail, $148 hauling passengers, and $146 handling express shipments. The railroad, which was shown to be an operating subsidiary of the Dierks Lumber & Coal Company, had $9115 in net operating income that year.

This activity lasted only two more years as in 1941, the Oklahoma & Rich Mountain Railroad applied for authority to abandon the entire line. On September 6, 1941 (some reports state that it was September 6, 1942, but ICC records show that it was 1941), the ICC granted authority to abandon the entire line, effective in 30 days. On September 20, 1941, the *Railway Age* magazine reported that the O&RM "has been authorized by Division 4 of the Interstate Commerce Commission to abandon as to interstate and foreign commerce its entire line extending from a connection with the Kansas City Southern at Page, Okla., westerly to Pine Valley, 16.9 miles." According to the Railroad Retirement Board, "Oklahoma & Rich Mountain Railroad Company coverage ceased November 23, 1941."

The town of Pine Valley had no reason to exist after the mill was closed and the tracks abandoned. Many of the buildings were removed and sold, with some hauled to other operations of Dierks Lumber, such as Wright City. The surrounding timberlands were sold to the U.S. Forest Service as part of the new Ouachita National Forest. A few concrete foundations and the shell of the concrete kilns still remain on private property. They can be seen on the west side of today's Muse, south of Oklahoma Highway

63 and to the east of county road N4625, also called River Road. Some of the railroad grades also still remain along the north bank of the Kiamichi River.

The station at Page, Oklahoma, located on the Kansas City Southern, was the outside connection for the Oklahoma & Rich Mountain Railroad. Little except the mainline of the KCS remains here, but this sign for the Page Cemetery still marks the location.

The Oklahoma & Rich Mountain Railroad was built between Page and Muse, both in Oklahoma, to serve the Pine Valley Lumber Company, owned by the Dierks Brothers. The primary facility of the lumber company was located about a mile south of Muse.

Grades of the Oklahoma & Rich Mountain Railroad can still be found near Muse, Oklahoma, where Dierks created the lumber community of Pine Valley.

Some of the large concrete structures of the Pine Valley Lumber Company still stand south of Muse, Oklahoma.

Not all of the structures that still stand are parts of the old Pine Valley Lumber sawmill. This small structure is reportedly the old jail.

Mountain Pine, Arkansas

For years, there were announcements that Dierks would extend the DeQueen & Eastern to Hot Springs, Arkansas. News reports about the planned railroad started by 1902, and the Arkansas Railroad Commission reported in 1905 that the DeQueen & Eastern was planning to build 100 miles of track from Provo northeast to Hot Springs, and that grading on 25 miles was already underway. Dierks had certainly looked at the timber around Hot Springs, and several logging lines were built northward from the mill at Dierks, but none ever reached Hot Springs.

Starting in 1922, Dierks began to purchase land and timber rights in Garland County, generally around Blakely Mountain to the northwest of Hot Springs. The town of Mountain Pine was planned as the location of a large sawmill, a company town, and the base of operations for a series of logging railroads. The townsite was chosen based upon a contract with Arkansas Power & Light (AP&L) to log the valleys that would be flooded by the new Blakely Mountain Dam, which created Lake Ouachita on the Ouachita River.

Construction of the new town of Mountain Pine began in January 1927 when land was cleared for the new sawmill (steel construction), houses, and a business district. Dierks Lumber & Coal announced that "the houses that we will build for our people will be modern and comfortable, and no less than 150 such homes will be included in the first part of the program....We will give them a modern church and school building. Then, too, they will have their own moving picture theatre for there must be a diversion, too. It will not be all work and no play." The town also included a company store (commissary) that provided food and supplies for the town's residents, and a company doctor who provided medical services for employees and their families. The $500,000+ sawmill started production in 1928, producing 165,000 board feet of lumber a day.

With more than 350 workers employed at the fifty-acre mill, Mountain Pine was the second-largest community in Garland County, behind Hot Springs, from the 1930s through the late 1970s. The Mountain Pine post office opened in 1927, and the town grew thanks to the local school system as well as the recreational activities at nearby Lake Ouachita and Lake Ouachita State Park.

A logging railroad first headed north into the valley of the Ouachita River. A logging community named Blakely was created near where Big Blakely and Little Blakely creeks flowed into the Ouachita River. The area had earlier been known as Cedar Glades, and a Blakely post office opened in 1936. By late 1937, the timber was cut and the logging community was moved to a new location. In 1940, a line was built to the northeast along Glazypeau Creek and Little Glazypeau Creek to Arkansas Highway 7 south of Blue Springs. The rail line then headed north on the east side of Highway 7 through Blue Springs to near the junction with Arkansas Highway 298. The rail line then turned to the northwest to Blakely, located west of Jessieville. This logging community became known as "Blakely Camp" or simply, "The Camp."

Blakely was described by many as a smaller version of the mill town at Mountain Pine. Dierks created housing that was rented to employees. There was also a company commissary, all provided electricity and water by the lumber company. Unlike Mountain Pine, Blakely didn't have its own school thanks to the nearby school at Jessieville. By this time, Dierks was using trucks to bring the logs from the woods to log yards along their rail lines. A log yard at Blakely featured a repair shop and fuel depot for log trucks, and also served as a temporary site for logs transported by truck from the woods. A daily train spotted empty log cars along the line and then brought the loaded cars back to Mountain Pine. Steam locomotives were used on the logging lines out of Mountain Pine until 1964. Maps show that the railroad remained until the late 1960s before trucks took over the movements of the timber to Mountain Pine.

By the late 1960s, the Dierks family was looking at selling their properties. One major sale in the Blakely area took place in 1969 when John Cooper of Cooper Communities acquired more than 20,000 acres that were owned by Dierks Forests. On the property, the firm created the gated retirement community named Hot Springs Village. Other things changed after Weyerhaeuser acquired the Dierks properties in 1969. Blakely remained a logging camp, but Weyerhaeuser almost immediately offered employees the opportunity to purchase their homes. The other company properties at Blakely, like the commissary, were also sold off, leaving just the log yard. The post office closed in

1997, and today Blakely is marked by four blocks of town on Blakely Camp Road.

For years, the Mountain Pine mill was served by Missouri Pacific, and then Union Pacific. This photo from 1991 shows Union Pacific local LRR47 passing the Mountain Pine City Limit sign while switching the mill.

Dierks and Weyerhaeuser also kept one or more of their locomotives at the Mountain Pine sawmill for switching and moving logs from its Blakely Camp. Here, locomotive D-21 is shown moving a string of Missouri Pacific wood chip cars into the mill.

In late 2001, Weyerhaeuser announced that it would begin closing its operations at Mountain Pine, and the mill finally closed in 2006. The complex has since been dismantled.

This highway sign for Blakely Camp Road marks the way to the former Dierks logging town of Blakely.

A few of the old Dierks logging buildings can still be found at Blakely, such as this abandoned house.

Forester, Arkansas

This is a little-known operation of Dierks, basically because it was originally built by the Caddo River Lumber Company in 1930. The operation was built by Thomas Whitaker "Whit" Rosborough, who had formed the Caddo River Lumber Company in 1906 at Rosboro, Arkansas. The Caddo River Lumber Company built a number of rail lines to log the woods around Glenwood and Norman, and to move the logs to the main sawmill at Rosboro. In 1924, Kansas City lumberman William F. Ingham bought into the firm. Ingham had long partnered with Dierks Lumber & Coal on lumber projects across the region. As the timber supply was used up, Rosborough looked for new areas to log. He found two areas, one in Oregon and one in western Arkansas southeast of Waldron in Scott County.

Reports from the time state that Caddo River Lumber moved its equipment to the new mill site by extending their logging railroad northward from Mauldin and across Mill Creek Mountain into the valley of the Fourche LaFave River. Everything from steam locomotives to log loaders to buildings were moved along this temporary rail line. Once everything was at Forester, Caddo River Lumber operated as many as six steam locomotives over 70 miles of standard gauge logging lines. Many of these were 2-6-2 and 2-8-2 locomotives with designs very similar to those used by the various Dierks rail operations.

The new lumber town was named after Waldron businessman Charles A. Forrester. The town was laid out in sections rather than streets. The main part was known as Green Town, and the second largest was called Angel Town. There was also Cannon Town, Water Tank Road, the Section Houses, and Happy Holler, the smallest section. The population of Forester in 1940 was 1306, including about 350 black residents living in their own section of rustic, red-stained houses called "the Quarters." They had their own school, church, and an entertainment center called the Barrel House, but shared the store, post office, and theater with the white residents.

The company provided houses, schools, churches, a theater, a post office, a drugstore, a barber/beauty shop, a twenty-eight-room hotel, a depot, a garage with car sales, a ballpark and stadium, a community hall/Masonic Lodge, and the company store. Forester had its own water system and power plant, and there was free healthcare for all, provided by a company-paid doctor. Forester had very little crime and only employed two town marshals in the twenty-year life of the town.

By the early 1930s, Dierks and Caddo River were the only large lumber companies operating in the Ouachita Mountains. The Forester mill became the largest and most productive in the state, with its huge lumber shed measuring eighty feet wide and 1000 feet long and storing millions of board feet of kiln-dried, planed lumber. Contractors logged for the mill with mule teams and wagons until 1940, when the company purchased trucks. The timber was brought to log yards where trains were used to haul the timber on to the log pond and mill at Forester. After all the largest timber was cut, Caddo River sold the town of Forester and the logging operations to Dierks Lumber & Coal on July 17, 1945. Reportedly, Dierks Lumber & Coal kept two steam engines at Forester to operate the log trains between the woods and the sawmill.

Dierks continued to operate the Forester mill until there was insufficient timber, adding a box factory and facilities to produce small blocks for toys, mop handles, and other consumer products. Originally, the purchase included about 2000 acres of owned land, plus the rights to cut timber on 22,000 acres of National Forest land that had been sold by Caddo River to the federal government. The rights to cut the government land lasted only four years and the few remaining Dierks' acres couldn't support the mill's operations. The end of the rail operations was underway by 1950 when Arkansas Highway 28 was paved most of the way to Forester and Dierks converted the field operations from rail to truck. In 1952, the mill closed and the whole town was moved or torn down, being sold to various companies and individuals. Some of the houses were moved to other towns where Dierks operated such as Mountain Pine, Dierks, and De Queen.

Forester is in an isolated part of the Ouachita Mountains, and this sign along Arkansas Highway 28 points the way to the small park that has developed there.

Although Forester, Arkansas, is no longer a community, this sign welcomes you to its former location, and the park, many ruins and historical signs that have replaced it.

The sawmill complex at Forester was once one of the largest in Arkansas. However, after the company's timber played out, Dierks had to bid for timber in the nearby national forests. When this became difficult to obtain in sufficient volumes, Dierks abandoned the mill and community at Forester. Several large concrete ruins remain more than seventy years later.

About the Author

Barton Jennings grew up in Arkansas, spending years in the Little Rock area exploring the various railroad lines across the state. During this time, De Queen was a popular stop, often photographing the Weyerhaeuser lines of the DeQueen & Eastern and the Texas, Oklahoma & Eastern. For almost three decades, Barton Jennings has been organizing charter passenger trains and writing the route descriptions, both for planning purposes and for the enjoyment of the passengers. These trips have been in all areas of the United States, often covering operations that haven't seen a passenger train in decades. One of these events was operating three days of trips over the DeQueen & Eastern and the Texas, Oklahoma & Eastern as part of the railroad's centennial event. This book is based upon these activities.

More than a dozen other books have come out of these experiences. In addition, Jennings has written a number of articles about various railroads for rail hobby magazines. His house has several rooms full of books, timetables and other documents about this and other railroads – important research items from a time long before today's internet. Today, Bart Jennings, after years working in the railroad industry, is a professor emeritus of supply chain management and teaches transportation operations. He also still teaches regulatory issues for the railroad industry, a way to stay in touch with the industry he loves.